10/22/16

M000203735

TED, PAT

YOUR SUCCESS IS
MY SUCCESS.
MANY THANKS FOR
YOUR ongoing TRUST
& SUPPORT.

FONDLY

Joel

SUCCESS MANIFESTO

Published by CelebrityPress®, Orlando, FL.

CelebrityPress® is a registered trademark.

Printed in the United States of America.

ISBN: 978-0-9975366-4-5
LCCN: 2016943774

This publication is designed to provide accurate and authoritative information with regard to the subject matter covered. It is sold with the understanding that the publisher is not engaged in rendering legal, accounting, or other professional advice. If legal advice or other expert assistance is required, the services of a competent professional should be sought. The opinions expressed by the authors in this book are not endorsed by CelebrityPress® and are the sole responsibility of the author rendering the opinion.

Most CelebrityPress® titles are available at special quantity discounts for bulk purchases for sales promotions, premiums, fundraising, and educational use. Special versions or book excerpts can also be created to fit specific needs.

For more information, please write:
CelebrityPress®
520 N. Orlando Ave, #2
Winter Park, FL 32789
or call 1.877.261.4930

Visit us online at: www.CelebrityPressPublishing.com

SUCCESS MANIFESTO

CelebrityPress®
Winter Park, Florida

CONTENTS

CHAPTER 1

THE POWER OF CHARISMA

BY BRIAN TRACY

Webster's Ninth New Collegiate Dictionary defines charisma as "a personal magic of leadership arousing special popular loyalty or enthusiasm for a public figure."

Charisma is also that special quality of magnetism that each person has and that each person uses to a certain degree. You have a special charisma to the people who look up to you, who respect and admire you—the members of your family and your friends and coworkers. Whenever and wherever a person feels a positive emotion towards another, he imbues that person with charisma, or attractiveness.

In trying to explain charisma, some people speak of an "aura." This aura is a light that is invisible to most people, but not to everyone, and that radiates out from a person and affects the people around that person in a positive or negative way. The halo around the heads of saints and mystics in many religious paintings was the artist's attempt to depict the light that people reported seeing around the heads of these men and women when they were speaking or praying, or in an intense emotional state.

You also have an aura around you that most people cannot see but that is there, nevertheless. This aura affects the way people react and respond to you, either positively or negatively. There is a lot that you can do, and a lot of good reasons for you to do it, to control this aura and make it work in your best interests.

If you're in sales, this aura, reflecting your level of charisma, can have a major impact on the way your prospects and customers treat you and deal with you. Top salespeople seem to be far more successful than the average salespeople in getting along with their customers. They're always more welcome, more positively received and more trusted than the others. They sell more, and they sell more easily. They make a better living, and they build better lives. Salespeople with charisma get far more pleasure out of their work and suffer far less from stress and rejection. The charismatic salesperson is almost invariably a top performer in his field and enjoys all the rewards that go with superior sales.

If you're in business, developing greater charisma can help you tremendously in working with your staff, your suppliers, your bankers, your customers and everyone else upon whom you depend for your success. People seem naturally drawn to those who possess charisma. They want to help them and support them. When you have charisma, people will open doors for you and bring you opportunities that otherwise would not have been available to you.

In your personal relationships, the quality of charisma can make your life more joyous, and happier. People will naturally want to be around you. Members of your family and your friends will be far happier in your company, and you will have a greater influence on them, causing them to feel better about themselves and to do better at the important things in their lives.

There is a close association between personal charisma and success in life. Probably 85 percent of your success and happiness will come from your relationships and interactions with others. The more positively others respond to you, the easier it will be for you to get the things you want.

In essence, when we discuss charisma, we are talking about the law of attraction. This law has been stated in many different ways down through the centuries, but it basically says that you inevitably attract into your life the people and circumstances that harmonize with your dominant thoughts.

In a sense, you are a *living magnet*, and you are constantly radiating thought waves, like a radio station radiates sound waves, that are picked up by other people. Your thoughts, intensified by your emotions, as radio waves are intensified by electric impulses, go out from you and are picked up by anyone who is tuned in to a similar wavelength. You then attract into your life people, ideas, opportunities, resources, circumstances and anything else that is consistent with your dominant frame of mind.

The law of attraction also explains how you can build up your levels of charisma so that you can have a greater and more positive impact on the people whose cooperation, support and affection you desire.

The critical thing to remember about charisma is that it is largely based on *perception*. It is based on what people think about you. It is not so much reality as it is what people perceive the reality of you to be. For example, one person can create charisma in another person by speaking in glowing terms about that person to a third party. If you believe that you are about to meet an outstanding and important person, that person will tend to have charisma for you at first sight.

One of the most charismatic people in the world was Mother Teresa of Calcutta. In a physical sense, she was a quiet, elderly, frail woman in poor health, and she wore a modest nun's habit. She might have been ignored by a person passing her on the street, were it not for the tremendous charisma she had developed and for the fact that her appearance was so well-known to so many people as a result.

If someone told you that he was going to introduce you to a brilliant, young self-made millionaire who was quiet and unassuming about his success, you would almost naturally imbue that person with charisma, and in his presence, you would act quite differently than you would if you had been told nothing at all. Charisma begins largely in the mind of the beholder.

Of course, lasting charisma depends more upon the person you *really* are than upon just the things you do. Nevertheless, you can build the perception of charisma for yourself by utilizing the ten great powers of personality that seem to have a major impact on the way that people think and feel about you.

The first of these powers is the power of *purpose*. Men and women with charisma and personal magnetism almost invariably have a clear vision of who they are, of where they're going and of what they're trying to achieve. Leaders in sales and management have a vision of what they're trying to create and why they're doing what they're doing. They're focused on accomplishing some great purpose. They're decisive about every aspect of their lives. They know exactly what they want and what they have to do to get it. They plan their work and work their plan.

In more than 3,300 studies of leadership, in every book and article ever written on leadership, the quality of purpose, or vision, was one of the few qualities that was consistently used in describing leaders.

You can increase your charisma and the magnetism of your personality by setting clear goals for yourself, making plans to achieve them, and working on your plans with discipline and determination every day. The whole world seems to move aside for the person who knows exactly where he is going. In fact, the clearer you are about your purposes and goals, the more likely people will be to attribute other positive qualities to you. They will see you, or perceive you, as being a better and more admirable human being. And when you have clear goals, you begin attracting to yourself the people and opportunities necessary to make those goals a reality.

The second personality power is *self-confidence*. Men and women with charisma have an intense belief in themselves and in what they are doing. They are usually calm, cool and composed about themselves and their work. Your level of self-confidence is often demonstrated in your courage, your willingness to do whatever is necessary to achieve a purpose that you believe in.

People are naturally attracted to those who exude a sense of self-confidence, those who have an unshakable belief in their ability to rise above circumstances to attain their goals.

One of the ways you demonstrate self-confidence is by assuming that people naturally like you and accept you and want to do business with you. For example, one of the most powerful ways to close a sale is simply to assume that the prospect has decided to purchase the product or service, and then go on to wrap up the details. One of the best ways to achieve success in your relationships is to assume that people naturally enjoy your company and want to be around you, and then proceed on that basis. The very act of behaving in a self-confident manner will generate personal charisma in the eyes of others.

The third power you can develop is enthusiasm. The more excited you are about accomplishing something that is important to you, the more excited others will be about helping you to do it. The fact is that emotions are contagious. The more passion you have for your life and your activities, the more charisma you will possess, and the more cooperation you will gain from others. Every great man or woman has been totally committed to a noble cause and, as a result, has attracted the support and encouragement of others—in many cases, thousands or millions of others.

The fourth personality power that you can develop is expertise, or competence. The more knowledgeable you are perceived to be in your field, the more charisma you will have among those who respect and admire that knowledge because of the impact it can have on their lives. This is also the power of excellence, of being recognized by others as an outstanding performer in your field. Men and women who do their jobs extremely well and who are recognized for the quality of their work are those who naturally attract the help and support of others. They have charisma.

The fifth power of personality that gives you charisma in the eyes of others is thorough preparation prior to undertaking any significant task. Whether you are calling on a prospect, meeting with your boss, giving a public talk or making any other kind of presentation, when you are well prepared, it becomes clear to everyone. The careers of many young people are put onto the fast track as a result of their coming to an important meeting after having done all their homework.

Whether it takes you hours or even days, if an upcoming meeting or interaction is important, take the time to get on top of your subject. Be so thoroughly prepared that nothing can faze you. Think through and consider every possibility and every ramification. Often, this effort to be fully prepared will do more to generate the respect of others than anything else you can do.

Remember that the power is always on the side of the person who has done the most preparation and has the best notes. Everything counts.

Leave nothing to chance. When you do something related to your work or career, take the time to do it right—in advance.

The sixth power that gives you charisma is *self-reliance*, or self-responsibility. The most successful men and women are intensely self-reliant. They look to themselves for the answers to their questions and problems. They never complain, and they never explain. They take complete ownership of projects. They volunteer for duties and step forward and accept accountability when things go wrong.

An amazing facet of human nature is that when you behave in a completely self-reliant manner, others will often be eager to help you achieve your goals. But if you seem to need the help and support of others, people will avoid you or do everything possible not to get involved with you.

One of the most admirable qualities of leaders, which lends a person charisma in the perception of others, is the capacity to step forward and take charge. The leader accepts complete responsibility for getting the job done, without making excuses and blaming anyone. When you become completely self-reliant, you experience a tremendous sense of control and power that enhances your feeling of well being and that generates the charisma that is so important to you in attracting the help of others.

The seventh personality power is *image*. There is both interpersonal image and intrapersonal image. Intrapersonal image, or self-image, is the way you see yourself and think about yourself in any situation. This self-image has an inordinate impact on the way you perform and on the way others see you and think about you. Your self-image plays an important part in your charisma.

The other type of image is *interpersonal*. This is the image or appearance that you convey to others. The way you look on the outside has an inordinate impact on the way people treat you and respond to you. Successful men and women are very aware of how they are coming across to others. They take a good deal of time to think through every aspect of their external appearance to assure that it is helping them rather than hurting them.

Remember that *everything counts*. If an element of your image is not building your charisma and your respect in the eyes of another person, it is probably lowering your charisma and your respect. Nothing is neutral. Everything is taken into the equation. Everything counts.

The three primary factors in personal appearance are clothes, grooming and accessories. Select your clothes with care. Before you go to an important meeting, stand in front of the mirror and ask yourself, "Do I look like one of the best people in my field?" If you don't feel that you look like one of the best people in your business, go back to the closet and change.

Look at the most successful people in your area of endeavor. What do they wear? How do they dress? How do they wear their hair? What kind of accessories do they use? Pattern yourself after the winners in your field, the people who already have personal magnetism and charisma. If you do what they do, over and over, you will eventually get the same results that they get.

The eighth form of personal power is *character*, or integrity. Men and women who possess the kind of charisma that arouses the enthusiastic support of others are invariably men and women with high values and principles. They are extremely realistic and honest with themselves and others. They have very clear ideals, and they continually aspire to live up to the highest that is in them. They speak well of people, and they guard their conversation, knowing that everything that they say is being remembered and recorded. They are aware that everything they do is contributing to the formation of their perception by others. Everything about their character is adding to or detracting from their level of charisma.

When you think of the most important men and women of any time, you think of men and women who aspired to greatness and who had high values for themselves and high expectations of others. When you make the decision to act consistent with the highest principles that you know, you begin to develop charisma. You begin to become the kind of person others admire and respect and want to emulate. You begin to attract into your life the help and support and encouragement of the kind of people you admire. You activate the law of attraction in the very best way.

The ninth power of personality is *self-discipline*, or self-mastery. Men and women of charisma are highly controlled. They have a tremendous sense of inner calm and outer resolve. They are well organized, and they demonstrate willpower and determination in everything they do.

The very act of being well organized, of having clear objectives and of having set clear priorities on your activities before beginning, gives you a sense of discipline and control. It causes people to respect and admire you. When you then exert your self-discipline by persisting in the face of difficulties, your charisma rating goes up.

Men and women who achieve leadership positions, who develop the perception of charisma in others, are invariably those who possess indomitable willpower and the ability to persist in a good cause until success is achieved. The more you persist when the going gets rough, the more self-discipline and resolve you develop, and the more charisma you tend to have.

The tenth power that you can develop, which underlies all of the other powers that lead to charisma, is *result-orientation*. In the final analysis, people ascribe charisma to those men and women who they feel can most enable them to achieve important goals or objectives.

We develop great perceptions of those men and women we can count on to help us achieve what is important to us. Men and women who make big sales develop charisma in the minds and hearts of their coworkers and superiors. They are spoken about in the most positive way. Men and women who are responsible for companies or departments that achieve high levels of profitability also develop charisma. They develop what is called the "halo effect." They are perceived by others to be extraordinary men and women who are capable of great things. Their shortcomings are often overlooked, while their strong points are overemphasized. They become charismatic.

Charisma actually comes from working on yourself. It comes from liking and accepting yourself unconditionally as you do and say the specific things that develop within you a powerful, charismatic personality.

When you set clear goals and become determined and purposeful, backing those goals with unshakable self-confidence, you develop charisma. When you are enthusiastic and excited about what you are doing, when you are totally committed to achieving something worthwhile, you radiate charisma. When you take the time to study and become an expert at what you do, and then prepare thoroughly for any opportunity to use your knowledge, skill or experience, the perception that others have of you goes straight up.

When you take complete responsibility and accept ownership, without making excuses or blaming others, you experience a sense of control that leads to the personal power that is the foundation of charisma. When you look like a winner in every respect, when you have the kind of external image that others admire, you build your charisma. When you develop your character by setting high standards and then disciplining yourself to live consistent with the highest principles you know, you become the kind of person who is admired and respected everywhere. You become the kind of person who radiates charisma to others. Finally, when you concentrate your energies on achieving the results that you have been hired to accomplish, the results that others expect of you, you develop the reputation for performance and achievement that inevitably leads to the perception of charisma.

You can develop the kind of charisma that opens doors for you by going to work on yourself, consistently and persistently, and becoming the kind of person everyone can admire and look up to. That's what charisma is all about.

About Brian

Brian Tracy is Chairman and CEO of Brian Tracy International, a company specializing in the training and development of individuals and organizations. Brian's goal is to help people achieve their personal and business goals faster and easier than they ever imagined.

Brian Tracy has consulted for more than 1,000 companies and addressed more than 5,000,000 people in 5,000 talks and seminars throughout the U.S.A., Canada and 70 other countries worldwide. As a Keynote speaker and seminar leader, he addresses more than 250,000 people each year.

For more information on Brian Tracy programs, go to:
• www.briantracy.com

CHAPTER 2

THE BIG GAME: GIVING LIFE YOUR BEST

BY LEIGH STEINBERG
Founder of Steinberg Sports

The foundation of all that we do is based on what our values and guiding principles are.

My father Warren raised me with two core values. First, it was important to treasure relationships, especially family. And second, I should make an impact in this world and help people who could not help themselves. Everything I am involved with, and create, relates back to these two priorities. It's not the money or fame which offer the ultimate test to the value of life—family, friendships, and being of service are what will fulfill you.

To achieve fulfillment in your life and career you need to gain clarity in respect to which values and goals are most critical to you. The only way to do this is through introspection.

It's not important what someone else thinks you should prioritize—only you know your heart and mind. Consider values like:

1. Short-term financial gain
2. Long-term financial security
3. Family and friends
4. Geographical location

5. Spiritual beliefs
6. Autonomy
7. Belief in what you do

Through a combination of these values and knowing yourself, you can be led to more fruitful decision making. And in my work in life, I have been driven by my understanding of this.

"ENTHUSIAST" TO REPRESENTATIVE

The best uses of our talents often come from the most unsuspecting moments.

I loved sports when I was growing up in Los Angeles; we had the Dodgers and Angels, Lakers and Rams, as well as SC and UCLA to root for. Going to these events created a bond between my father, my brothers, and I—just like it does for others—including people from disparate backgrounds.

When I began to contemplate the career that I would like, I chose law. I wanted to be a criminal attorney or District Attorney. To pursue this, I attended UCLA and Cal Berkeley for undergraduate and law school.

I worked as a grad counselor in an undergraduate dorm which happened to be the one in which the football team resided. One of the students was the Cal Quarterback Steve Bartkowski, who became the number one overall draft pick in the 1975 NFL draft, taken by the Atlanta Falcons, and he asked me to represent him. This was at a time when there was no established field of sports representation, but I agreed to do it. Ultimately, we negotiated the largest contract in the history of the NFL and flew back to Atlanta to sign the contract.

There were klieg lights at the airport and a crowd pressed up against a police line. We heard a reporter say: "We interrupt the Johnny Carson show to present a special live interview with Steve and his attorney Leigh." At that moment, I realized how athletes were the movie stars and celebrities of their communities.

I saw a way to implement the values I was raised with by working with athletes.

You may find yourself involved in a field in the future that does not even exist presently, so flexibility is key. Being flexible and being aware helped guide me to this opportunity, and ever since I have been able to use my passion to unlock incredible amounts of energy and excitement about what I do and who I help. It is less work than a lifestyle.

Athletes have a unique opportunity to serve as role models and trigger imitative behavior. Helping them recognize this requires specific steps, which include: retracing their roots, and establishing scholarship funds and charitable foundations in their high school, collegiate, and professional communities. This is done to leave a legacy and enhance the quality of life of others.

GUIDING ATHLETES TOWARD THEIR GREATER GOOD

*The powerful voice of an athlete can only be surpassed
by the power of their actions.*

As the years passed, I was able to represent 61 first-round draft picks in the NFL, 8 of whom were the first pick overall, and 8 who have entered the Hall of Fame. We have also developed a large practice in Major League Baseball, the NBA, boxing, and Olympic sports. Regardless of the sport, the key to fulfilling an athlete is to help them understand his or her greatest fears and anxieties, and their greatest hopes and dreams. This can only be done by creating a climate of trust and rapport with an athlete so he will open up and reveal himself.

CAREFUL LISTENING BECAME THE MOST IMPORTANT PART OF THIS PROCESS.

Peeling back the layers of the onion to truly bond in a deep way with another person is the core of this approach. Can you put yourself in the heart and mind of another human being and see the world the way they see it? This one skill will allow you to navigate life successfully.

As mentioned earlier, an athlete must evaluate which priorities and values are of significance to them, and to do this requires introspection. In addition to the universal values, concepts like being a starter, playing for a winning team, the quality of coaching, and the offensive or defensive scheme come into play. To get through all these layers you must possess a deep understanding of another person's priorities in order to successfully represent them.

In 1975, professional sport was in an embryonic state compared to the present. Having vision and an ability to see the future became central to building our business. It was clear that television was about to explode from its stagnant stage of three networks to one where there were hundreds. This meant that exponentially more actual games, highlights, features, and analysis programming would be shown. Because sports delivers a guaranteed audience that will not risk recording games, this onset triggered a bonanza in rights fees. NFL teams that received $2 million as their share of the national television contract in 1976, received $226 million in 2015. New stadia were on the horizon with luxury boxes, premium seating, expanded signage, and sponsorship and naming rights. In addition, memorabilia, merchandising, fantasy sports, and multiple platforms of content supply catapulted franchise values. Case in point— the Dallas Cowboys were purchased for $140 million in 1989, they currently are valued at $4 billion.

Being able to visualize the future allowed me to establish the first Internet site which featured athletes, back in 1998. Players like Troy Aikman, Michael Jordan, and Ken Griffey Jr. wrote weekly diaries and discussed their charitable foundations. This platform gave fans an opportunity to follow athletes they admired and purchase merchandise directly from them. We ran the site out of our offices and sold control to venture capitalists for a huge multiple in several years. This same type of vision also enabled my firm to launch projects like sports-themed motion pictures and television shows, apps for the Internet, plus health and safety products in which we could take an equity position.

My father imbued a strong sense of personal responsibility into me. He used to say, "If you see a problem or concern and wait for 'they' or 'them' to address it, you can wait forever. You are the 'they', son, the 'they' is you."

My visions for the potential of athletes if given the proper representation had provided me great joy. However, since my business was built on my core values, I found myself in a crisis of conscience.

In the 1980s, our agency represented about half the starting quarterbacks in the NFL at one time. There was a reoccurring theme—they kept getting knocked out during games. I knew this could not be healthy for long term brain function and it concerned me. Always one to take action on my concerns, we held the first Concussion Seminar in Newport Beach in 1994. This seminar gave players access to insight from leading neurologists that explained the dangers and issued that stemmed from concussions. Afterward, a white paper was even sent to every NFL team. They ignored it… But I could not.

What was the proper way to insure that I was not passively involved in enabling clients down the road to dementia?

It took a decade to get to the next stage, but we held another seminar in 2005. This time it was in conjunction with the Concussion Institute. The neurologists reported that three or more concussions can occasion an exponentially higher rate of ALS, premature senility, chronic traumatic encephalopathy, and depression. The message was received—a little— but still not enough from my perspective. Since then I have worked to promote safer helmetry, rules changes, training camp and practices which are contact free, and nutraceuticals and pharmaceuticals which promote healing.

Something else that concerned me was that my generation would be the first to hand down a degraded quality of life to our kids due to climate change. It was another opportunity to present to athletes so they could show their socially-conscious side. We promoted a Sporting Green Alliance to aggregate sustainable technology in wind, solar, recycling, resurfacing, and water to take to stadia, arenas, and practice fields at the high school, collegiate, and professional level. The goal was to drop carbon emissions and energy costs and transform the venues into educational platforms so fans could see how to incorporate these concepts into their own homes and businesses.

In the wake of the Oklahoma City terrorist bombing, I became concerned that skinheads and hate groups were in the ascendancy. In conjunction with the Anti-Defamation League, we created a training program, Steinberg Leadership, to provide skilled leaders in the fight against hate. Young professionals took a year of training in how to spot hate groups and aid local police departments. They learned how to intervene in crisis situations and promote ethnic tolerance in schools. It spread to thirty cities with many thousands of volunteers—the advance vanguard against hate.

Few people can do as much to change the world for the better than an athlete that understands the obligation that comes with their celebrity status. Our agency has helped guide 122 players to establish scholarship funds, or aid a church or youth group in their hometown community. Players like Troy Aikman, Edgerrin James, and Steve Young established scholarships at their universities. Running back Warrick Dunn's "Homes for the Holidays" has put 145 single mothers and their families into the first home they would ever own, by making the down payment and furnishing the homes.

Athletes have the ability to permeate the perceptual screen that rebellious adolescents erect against authority figures and stimulate behavior change. When Lennox Lewis, the heavyweight boxing champion, appeared in a public service announcement proclaiming: "Real Men Don't Hit Women," it did more in the fight against domestic violence than 100 authority figures could do. Or quarterback Steve Young and middleweight boxing champion Oscar de La Hoya stressing: "Prejudice is Foul Play."

The effectiveness of all these initiatives all start with listening and getting to know the athlete. There is no better way to understand their values and priorities so you can help them use their talents for something that extends beyond their sport.

USING TODAY TO CULTIVATE A BETTER TOMORROW
We all have constant reminders of why we should live our best life.

One of the most exciting moments that an NFL representative can have is NFL Draft Night. It's a celebration of the new and the energy is second to no other that I've ever experienced. This year, as I stood next to new Denver Broncos quarterback Paxton Lynch on NFL Draft Night 2016, I felt all of this coalesce in one joyous moment. Values, self-awareness, listening skills, and passion: My personal responsibility to create a life worth living.

About Leigh

Leigh Steinberg, the world's first "super agent," founded his sports law practice in 1975 when he negotiated a then-record contract for the first overall pick in the NFL draft Steve Bartkowski. Since then, Leigh has solidified his name as one of the premiere player representatives in all of sports, and specifically the NFL where he represented a record eight different number-one NFL draft picks, over 60 first-round draft picks, and consistently negotiated record-breaking contracts. His past clients include NFL stars and Hall of Famers Troy Aikman, Steve Young, Warren Moon, Drew Bledsoe, Ben Roethlisberger, Thurman Thomas, Ricky Williams, Derrick Thomas, Edgerrin James, Jevon Kearse, and Bruce Smith, boxing legends Lennox Lewis and Oscar De La Hoya, and a plethora of NBA, MLB, and Olympic athletes. In all, Leigh has negotiated over a billion dollars in NFL contracts, and over two billion dollars in athlete contract and endorsement deals.

Driven by the philosophy that professional athletes possess the cultural influence to reach the masses and have a significant social impact, Leigh has helped his clients to become valuable members of their communities and to be models for imitative behavior. Specifically, Leigh has helped his clients develop over a hundred charitable foundations, which have raised over $700 million for innumerable causes. Leigh challenges his players to find a cause which they feel passionate about and fight for it. For example, Rolf Benirschke's "Kicks for Critters" helped fund protection of endangered species and Warrick Dunn's "Homes for the Holidays" gives single parents the opportunity to own a home for the first time in their lives.

Leigh created the Steinberg Leadership Program with the Human Relations Commission of Orange County to give leadership and tolerance training to high school and middle school leaders in a series of one-week camps. Leigh also, has three Presidential commendations for community service.

Leigh has been named Man of the Year over a dozen times by a diverse group of organizations that include the March of Dimes, Cedars Sinai, the Southern California Boy Scouts, the Orange County and Los Angeles Human Relations Commissions, the Orange County and Los Angeles divisions of the Anti-Defamation League. Leigh has been awarded the "Keys to the City" of five cities: San Francisco, CA, Memphis, TN, Jacksonville, FL, Concord, CA and Indianapolis, IN.

An accomplished speaker, Steinberg has traveled the world addressing topics ranging from sports and entertainment to political and economic issues. In 1992, Steinberg helped lead a successful campaign to prevent the San Francisco Giants baseball club from relocating to Florida. For his efforts, then San Francisco Mayor Frank Jordan honored him by declaring "Leigh Steinberg Day" in the city of SF soon after.

Leigh is often credited as the inspiration for the Oscar-winning film *Jerry Maguire*. In addition to receiving a production credit for the movie, Leigh also consulted on features such as *Any Given Sunday, For Love of the Game,* and *Arli$$.*

In 1994, then Oakland Mayor Elihu Harris utilized Steinberg as a consultant in his successful bid to prevent the Oakland Athletics baseball club from relocating to Sacramento or San Jose. Steinberg also served as co-chairperson of the "Save the Rams" committee. Leigh Steinberg has also been active in pursuits to attract a new football franchise to locate in Los Angeles.

Leigh has been rated the #6 Most Powerful Person in the NFL according to "Football Digest" and the #16 Most Powerful Person in Sports according to "Sporting News."

Leigh wrote a best-selling book in 1998, *Winning with Integrity,* a New York Times best seller, providing readers insight on how to improve their life through non-confrontational negotiating. He also wrote, *The Agent,* published in 2014.

CHAPTER 3

DON'T LET THE PEPPERMINT GO!

BY BRANDON NELSON

There is one thing that is true about human beings. We love shortcuts! Everyone wants to know what the path of least resistance is. Which route is the fastest? How can I beat the traffic? How can I bypass the huge workload in front of me? Even those who have learned not to fall into the "shortcut" trap had to fight the urge to get around the dirty word. Do you know what that word is? Work! We completely underestimate the amount of work, effort, sweat, and energy it takes to become the huge success we fantasize about.

This is something that was evident in my life. I loved to use clichés like, "I'm going to work smarter and not harder." I would try to skirt around the dirty work by utilizing the "law of attraction" and fool myself into thinking that I was 'gonna' meditate for a few moments, close my eyes, and BAM! I would magically appear on large stages across the globe, featured in magazines, and on every major television network with no hard work involved. Boy, was I under a strong delusion! The only magic happening in my life was the disappearing act the money in my bank account would do on a consistent basis. Seriously. I had become completely out of touch with reality and was numb to the fact that my life was nowhere that I thought it would be.

Some of you may have found (or find) yourself in this position. Stuck, without any hint of light at the end of the tunnel. We live in a society of instant gratification. People simply do not respect the process anymore.

However, in order to be great, we must go through the processes of life and allow them to cultivate the greatness that lies within each and every one of us. As a matter of fact, you should put your hand on your heart right now and say to yourself, "I am great." You have to tell yourself that until you believe it. Do not be discouraged by the process. It is necessary for our development and is the doorway to the marvelous life we want to experience.

Everything has a process. I remember growing up, my grandmother would have me sing at every event she could possibly place me in. That started when I was around five. I remember standing on the stage in front of all these people and having to sing songs. I did pretty well, cou-pled with the fact that I was quite the stud in those days! I recall being in church choirs at nine and ten years of age. I had the range of a soprano back then. I could belt out notes like it was nothing. Those were fun times. Then, the unthinkable happened. (Dun! Dun! Dun!!!) Puberty! My voice dropped like a sack of hammers. I couldn't sing a note if my mom's life depended upon it. As I look back, I often wonder if all the people who were telling me how great of a singer I was at that time were just lying to spare the feelings of a young adolescent. Whatever the case, my life was over. My confidence was shattered. It was a problem that I felt I could not overcome. Little did I know, I was simply just going through the process. The process of becoming something better than I once was. I could not see it because I was focused on the problem. I was feeling sorry for myself and angry about the things that were not going my way. Singing competitions at school were tough. I struggled tremendously.

My last year of high school, I began to search for a solution. I was reading anything I could about the human voice. I devoured hours and hours of articles and videos pertaining to singing. Little did I know, I was on my way to becoming a professional in my field. The more I learned, the more I applied to my singing. Progress was being made, even if it was little by little. For the first time in years, I was starting to believe that all was not lost. I must stress again, things did not come together all at once. Through the process, I was learning to overcome this obstacle that at one time in my life seemed far too difficult for me to conquer.

Looking back (now many years removed) on that awkward and tough patch of my life, I can smile about it all. I find joy in the process. I am thankful for what I learned and what I experienced. The hard work, the embarrassment, the perseverance, it all paid off. And I want you to know that your labor is not in vain. Do not give up. Do not make a permanent decision in a temporary circumstance. Learn to push through and keep your eyes on the final destination. You have something in you that's greater than what you could ever think or imagine. This isn't just some 'pie-in-the-sky' inspirational talk. You have to see yourself in a better position than the one you are in right now. You have to believe in yourself when no one else does.

There is an old Hindu adage that goes something like this:

"...there was once a time when all human beings were gods, but they so abused their divinity that Brahma, the chief god, decided to take it away from them and hide it where it could never be found.

Where to hide their divinity was the question. So Brahma called a council of the gods to help him decide. "Let's bury it deep in the earth," said the gods. But Brahma answered, "No, that will not do because humans will dig into the earth and find it." Then the gods said, "Let's sink it in the deepest ocean." But Brahma said, "No, not there, for they will learn to dive into the ocean and will find it." Then the gods said, "Let's take it to the top of the highest mountain and hide it there." But once again Brahma replied, "No, that will not do either, because they will eventually climb every mountain and once again take up their divinity." Then the gods gave up and said, "We do not know where to hide it, because it seems that there is no place on earth or in the sea that human beings will not eventually reach."

Brahma thought for a long time and then said, "Here is what we will do. We will hide their divinity deep in the center of their own being, for humans will never think to look for it there."

All the gods agreed that this was the perfect hiding place, and the deed was done. And since that time humans have been going up and down the earth, digging, diving, climbing, and exploring – searching for something already within themselves."

This is a powerful (fictional) story that shows how we doubt the potential that is in us. Look back over your life for a moment. Think of the progress that you have made. How far you have come. You can look back on it with joy. The process has made you who you are today and brought you to this point. And it will continue to lead you into further success. Do not live in doubt and self-pity. Never downplay the process. It is making you into the person you want to become.

When I decided to branch off from music and delve into the world of investments, I had no idea what I was getting myself into. And much like the miserable period of my awkward, puberty-ruined, teenage voice, I once again found myself overwhelmed by the reality of my own inadequacy. I knew nothing about investing. I was not rich. How in the world would I ever be able to grab the attention of the ultra-wealthy and gain their trust. I wanted these people to invest millions of dollars with me. I do not like to ask people for one dollar, much less a million. Don't get me wrong, I truly believed in my product. I was solving a problem that many investors come face-to-face with on a daily basis. Not only was my investment opportunity safe, but it also yielded an incredible R.O.I. (Return on Investment.) I had a product that would gain my clients a whopping sixty-five percent fixed R.O.I. That is incredible! However, the magnitude of my product was not enough to pry my mind away from the feelings of being in way over my head. Do you know what that sounds like? It sounds like life was bringing on the process again, baby!

I had to draw on the strength from the victories I had enjoyed in my past. I had to remember the difficult times that I had already come through. I had to once again find the joy in the process. The joy of my desire fulfilled. My grandparents have a Yorkie named Bentley. He is among the cutest of dogs. He is also among the meanest of dogs. I have never met any creature that suffers from "little man" syndrome quite like he does. When he was a puppy, he would often times get ahold of things that he had no business getting ahold of. He would hide himself underneath the living room table and would become suspiciously quiet. One particular day, I noticed his sneaky tail under the table. He was chewing on what seemed to be a peppermint. Where he found a peppermint I will never know. I knelt down and reached my hand to grab the mint. Big mistake! Bentley bit the living daylights out of my hand. At that moment, I realized that confiscating this mint was going to be a more daunting task than I had initially thought. For the next five minutes, I used every technique possible to get this delicious piece of candy away from the grips of a seven pound dog.

We need to learn to approach our goals with the same tenacity that Bentley has! (Yes, I am using the dog to get my point across.) He knew what he wanted and was unwilling to let it go without a fight. We must grab ahold of our dreams, goals, visions and aspirations; and we must do all we can to see them through. We must fight off the enemies of worry, fear, doubt, intimidation, etc. That is truly what the process is about. It teaches us that we really do possess what it takes to see our dreams come true. We are powerful creatures and the process brings that fact into reality for the world to see. It will seem like an overnight success to most, but you will know that it was a long, tedious, strenuous process that brought you to the point of massive results. The day I hit a billion dollars in investments for my clients, there is going to be a grand celebration. And I will be able to look back on the process with joy. Not just with joy due to my accomplishments, but joy about the future. It will only get better. Your best is ahead of you. Declare that over your life! Say, "My best is ahead of me."

Here are a few things I would like you to take away from this chapter. They are very simple:

1. Realize the process
2. Embrace the process
3. Learn from the process
4. Believe in the process
5. Commit to the process
6. Enjoy the process

Do not wander around in a state of defeat. Every obstacle . . . Every road-block . . . Every challenge . . . It is all a part of the process and is all necessary in the pursuit of the life that you want to live. Remember, the process doesn't come to destroy you, but it comes to produce the type of person that doesn't just have victory as an experience, but as lifestyle. Be encouraged! Move forward today in power and might. And pretty soon you will be telling your story and inspiring others with what you have accomplished! Grab the peppermint and don't let go!

About Brandon

Brandon Nelson is emerging as one of the most inspirational and encouraging voices of today. What started as a young boy singing in small churches in Louisiana, Brandon's music career grew rapidly. He found himself on stages every week singing to thousands of people and inspiring them through his music. He has shared the stage with many of today's high profile speakers and recording artists.

Brandon is the founder of N.W.O. Global, a company that exists to empower people to experience life to the fullest. They offer a variety of life-coaching material as well as a life settlement division that is geared towards helping seniors get financial value from their life insurance policies.

Re-think Investments, also founded by Brandon, is a company that provides accredited investors with a powerful life share investment product that yields a 65% R.O.I.

Brandon was selected as one of America's CelebrityExperts®. He continues to travel the country speaking and bringing hope to countless people. In 2014, He began pastoring Level Ground Church in Groves, TX. He has a podcast that can be heard weekly.

You can connect with Brandon at:

Brandon@nwoutlook.com
Facebook.com/BrandonNelsonBiz/

CHAPTER 4

THE MOST VALUABLE COMPANY IN THE WORLD MAY BE YOURS!

BY RON EVERETT
Business Valuation Center

However beautiful the strategy, you should
occasionally look at the results.
~ Winston Churchill

You have a nice business and it's going good. Maybe even ready to explode in growth, leaving you with the critical decision: Do I take on this growth myself or sell my company to someone more capable? Decisions like this are tough. Like the stocks in your personal portfolio, the value of your business goes up or down every day due to a number of factors, some of which you can control and others which you cannot. So, regardless of when you ultimately decide to sell your company, how do you make sure the value of your company is always increasing – or hopefully, multiplying?

It's estimated that on average about 80% of a typical business owner's net worth is tied up in the value of the business. But most owners have no idea what their most valuable asset is worth, nor how to make it worth more in the acquisition marketplace. Most owners would be very surprised to learn that creating value is not simply a matter of increasing revenues and earnings and showing better historical performance. In fact, over the past decade, the valuation game has dramatically changed. Based on our extensive experience in researching over 5,000 transactions in many industries, there's an important lesson to be learned about market behavior in today's Innovation Economy:

INVESTORS PAY FAR MORE FOR A COMPANY'S FUTURE - THAN ITS PAST.

Unfortunately, most businesses are sold based on their last twelve month's financial results. If there is reasonable certainty that growth will continue, then the buyer has created a value windfall for himself on the day of closing. A portion of that windfall rightfully belongs in the seller's pocket. This is the reason why most business owners ultimately sell their company for far less than its fair market value. Owners typically focus on "selling" past performance instead of creating a believable version of the future that reflects predictable growth. Astute buyers focus on a company's history only to justify reasons to decrease its value – never to justify a premium. Astute sellers focus on building a believable future strategy that increases the company's value *today*.

This shift in marketplace psychology could generate *trillions* of dollars in new value for owners. This phenomenon is quite obvious in certain market segments of the Innovation Economy – for example, take companies like Uber, Airbnb, SpaceX and Snapchat. They're called "unicorns" – private companies valued at $1 billion or more. The billion-dollar technology startup was once the stuff of legend and myth. Today they're seemingly everywhere, backed by a bull market and a new generation of disruptive technology. The unicorns illustrate the result of this market behavior to the extreme – but the underlying premise that a credible future vision creates far more value in the marketplace than historical performance is true for all viable businesses - not just for the unicorns.

In the merger and acquisition world, we talk a lot about earnings multiples. For instance, one is the Price to Earnings multiple or "P/E" multiple – "short-cut" ways of valuing companies that are often relied upon in negotiations by both buyers and sellers.

Obviously, as a seller, you'd prefer a higher multiple to be applied to your earnings than a lower one. Why then would anyone pay a higher P/E multiple for your company versus a similar competitor? The answer is simple: Because future earnings don't stay constant.

The fact that some companies in the same industry sector have P/E multiples of 30x and others have P/E multiples of 3x tells you that investors (buyers) are willing to take substantial gambles on the potential of improved future earnings of some companies, while quite skeptical of others. *The buyer's focus on the future represents an unprecedented opportunity for business owners to create significant value by simply building a credible vision of the future.* However, most owners are either unwilling or unable to paint a picture of the future of their company that is more valuable than its past – and, sadly, the true fair market value of their most valuable asset is never achieved. Yet, it should be noted that in high-growth industries, it is quite common for 90% or more of a company's purchase price to be predicated on future expectations. For this reason, there is an incredible monetary incentive for the owner to create a credible future scenario for the company, where the buyer can envision himself achieving the strategic vision of the seller.

Twenty years ago, it was difficult to establish any credible business value without several years of financial history. And, factor in that it usually took two years to get your product done, another two years to get it to market, and then finally, in the next two years, you finally might see some revenue and earnings growth and it starts looking like your company could be valuable and saleable.

In today's business environment, the cycle is considerably more fast-paced. It goes something like this:

- You have an idea and start a company.
- Your time to market is fast (2-18 months).
- You don't need funding.
- Your go-to-market plan is established with early adopters.
- Your valuation is driven by future projections.
- Intellectual property and intangible assets have significant value.
- A medium-to-large sized company buys the business for relatively high value.
- The buyer grows the business generating high returns.
- Your exit time is anywhere from 1.5 years to 5 years.
- The low (or no) dilution for founders and owners creates a high return.

Prospective buyers want to buy your business for four main reasons:
- To capture new markets that are growing faster than their own.
- To protect their own market from erosion due to competition.
- To own intellectual property that protects competitive advantages.
- To get smart employees who make them more competitive.

WHAT'S YOUR "GROW BIG FAST" STRATEGY?

Dream big, get it done, speed it up.
~ Tony Robbins

Business owners and CEOs are drawn to the stories they hear about other businesses – stories that share how a company's value is multiplied by substantial amounts, seemingly overnight. Stories about Google, Apple, Ebay and Facebook are teasers, making you wonder if your business will be the next big one to achieve "unicorn" status.

Maximum Acquisition Value is achievable by every business owner willing to embrace a new view of their business world.

Peter Theil, co-founder of PayPal and Palantir, and author of *Zero to One: Notes on Startups, or How to Build the Future*, expressed this view:

"Think about how your industry has changed over the past decade. We now have access to all the basic building blocks at incredibly low cost – connectivity, computing, manufacturing, distribution, talent – so it no longer takes thousands of people and hundreds of offices to create a company with significant value, global reach and market impact. 'Scaling' – namely a hyper-growth business strategy – needs to be the core part of your business plan. Competition is much more intense these days and competitive advantages can disappear overnight, so you have to have a 'grow-big-fast' strategy."

The fact is - most companies don't have a 'grow-big-fast' strategy - and that's why **ValueX3**^{SM} was created - a powerful strategy building process for growing and capturing *Maximum Acquisition Value*. We've distilled our collective observations, insights and processes into a breakthrough program: **ValueX3**^{SM}. In this highly valuable process, we first determine your company's current value and future *Maximum Acquisition Value* - and then construct the tools, processes and road map to get you there.

Most CEOs fail to achieve *Maximum Acquisition Value* because of three fundamental blind spots in their thinking:

1. They don't know what's truly driving the value of the most successful companies in their industry.
2. They don't know the value creation processes to extract hyper-value from their company's untapped intellectual property and hidden intangible assets.
3. They don't know the profile of the ideal strategic buyer - *and what he's really looking for* - that creates *Maximum Acquisition Value*.

ValueX3^{SM} provides you with direct answers to these three questions that every CEO should be asking:

1. What's my company's current market value?
2. What's my company's *Maximum Acquisition Value* if I extract all potential value from its intellectual property and intangible assets?
3. What changes does my company need to make to attract a strategic buyer willing to pay *Maximum Acquisition Value*?

Without solid, credible answers to these three pressing questions, the ability to create exponential value growth from where your business is today, is more likely an unachievable dream.

CREATING MAXIMUM ACQUISITION VALUE

In the chart below there are 18 value drivers focused on the market (external drivers), and operations (internal drivers), and each is important to all businesses, albeit unknown to a good share of business owners. By putting emphasis and focus on these drivers, a business can take immediate steps toward achieving its Maximum Acquisition Value.

ValueX3 Value Drivers	
9 External Drivers	**9 Internal Drivers**
Market Growth	Strategic Leadership
Market Size	Business Model
Market Share	Financial
Revenue Composition	Marketing
Market Barriers	Operations
Differentiation	Innovation
Brand Awareness	Management Team
Quality of Earnings	Intellectual Property
Customers	Customer Satisfaction

This assessment allows an owner to delve much deeper into their company's true value. Then, we are better able to communicate a company's performance relative to each driver, and suggest the appropriate tasks to improve performance with the objective of achieving Maximum Acquisition Value within three to six months.

CASE STUDIES OF HOW VALUEX3^{SM} WORKS TO CREATE MAXIMUM ACQUISITION VALUE

Growth is never by mere chance; it is the result of forces working together.
~James Cash Penney

How **ValueX3**^{SM} *Turned A Claims Processor Into An IT Company — And Brought The Owners 400% More In Value*

One recent client was the largest health insurance claims processor in Maryland. A claims processing company is viewed by many acquirers as an unattractive and very price competitive business, providing low margin administrative services to insurance companies. Yet, their clients were substantial companies like Blue Cross/Blue Shield, Aetna, and Cigna. The company was designed to process claims cheaper, better, and faster than their clients could do it internally. They could perform these services at an efficient cost because they had developed a file conversion technology that could be utilized with any client's internal files. This was a very valuable intangible asset that would be highly prized by the marketplace and the competition – if only the market and competition knew about it. Our analysis revealed the actual reason for their success, and w*e convinced the owners to present their company to the acquisition marketplace as a healthcare information technology company instead of a claims processing firm.* Their valuation skyrocketed from an initial offer of $6 million as a claims processing company to an ultimate closing acquisition price of $24 million, 4-times higher as a healthcare IT company.

The Case Of The "Big Data" Company And How **ValueX3**^{SM} *Helped Them Skyrocket Their Valuation By 300%*

We recently had the opportunity to perform a valuation engagement for a Government IT company called PSI. At the time, the company had decided, that based on their existing valuation, it was "not a good time to sell". They believed they could not realize their acquisition price objective by selling the company in the current market. We processed the company through ValueX3^{SM} and, based on our guidance and recommendations, we repackaged the company from being just another Government IT contractor into a "Big Data" technology company. Based on this one change in market perception, we were able to sell the company to a South Korean investment syndicate for over 3-times the original valuation.

VALUE CREATION CAN START TODAY

Growth is never by mere chance; it is the result of forces working together.
~ James Cash Penney

What is your next stage? Are you ready to move on to bigger challenges, start another company or retire? At Business Valuation Center, our experience in value-building helps business owners and CEOs recognize the most impactful strategies to create Maximum Acquisition Value for their current situation, or if they plan to sell years later. Whatever your next stage may be, there is a path to multiply value that can be uncovered with ValueX3^{SM}.

About Ron

Ron Everett, CBA, CVA, has served as a merger and acquisition advisor and corporate valuation expert to over 3,500 companies. He is a co-founder and Managing Partner of his current firm, Business Valuation Center, and also leads the firm's Global Equity Partnership Program. Over the past 25 years, Ron has held positions as New England Director of Valuation Services for Ernst & Young, Partner and National Director of the Technology Valuation Practice for CBIZ, a large publicly-held professional services firm, and President of a regional business valuation firm. He has specialized expertise in conducting fairness and solvency opinions, in addition to pricing companies for purchase or sale, initial public offerings, private placements, and recapitalizations.

Mr. Everett's background includes many years of valuation consulting and merger and acquisition (M&A) advisory services to the owners of manufacturing, service and distribution businesses. These engagements include: capital stock, purchase price allocations, purchased "in process" R&D, sale price determination, SEC "cheap stock", performance improvement programs, merger and acquisition analyses, offering memorandums, IRS gift and estate tax planning and filings, family limited partnerships (FLP), valuation studies, fractional real estate interests, premium and discount studies, stockholder dispute arbitration, expert testimony and litigation support. He also has extensive experience in the valuation of intangible assets, including: patents, developed technology, software, databases, trademarks, trade names, licenses, contracts, backlog, distribution rights, customer lists, leases, royalty agreements, franchises, debt instruments and non-compete agreements.

His firm, Business Valuation Center (BVC) was also the exclusive valuation advisor to the U.S. Small Business Administration's SBIC Program, which is the largest fund of venture capital and private equity funds in the world, with over $24 billion under management. Ron was the Project Director for all SBIC valuations performed by Business Valuation Center, and has personally "signed off" on over 1,500 valuation opinions for the Federal Government as a precondition to private equity funds (SBICs) receiving additional investment funding for their portfolio companies from the U.S. Treasury. In addition to valuing over 1,500 companies for the SBA, BVC was also selected to conduct an independent review and author a report on the SBA's Small Business Investment Company (SBIC) valuation guidelines. Nearly all of BVC's recommendations were adopted by the SBA, recognizing BVC as an unparalleled business valuation authority in the United States on private equity valuation—having literally re-written and modernized the valuation standards used by the Federal Government.

Ron has also directed valuations and solvency opinions for over 200 private equity firms, including top tier investment firms such as Summit Partners, Advent International and Thomas H. Lee Partners, as well as many large banking institutions, including Wells Fargo, Bank of America and Credit Suisse. He is a Certified Business Appraiser (CBA) and Certified Valuation Analyst (CVA), and a member of the Institute of Business Appraisers and the National Association of Certified Valuation Analysts.

CHAPTER 5

NIFTY TO BE THRIFTY AT AGE FIFTY

– BEFORE AND AFTER . . . AND THEN WHAT?

BY JOEL N. GREENBERG

The age of baby boomer dominance is now upon us, and with this phenomenon comes the perils of overspending and inadequate retirement savings.

Classic cries of . . . "If we knew then, what we know now..." . . . are constantly being voiced. Just think how much better our financial situation could be as we race towards the next chapter of our "golden years"!

Having been in the financial services industry since 1978, I've had the good fortune of working with many successful, everyday people. Mom and Pop businesses, your neighbors next door, people who have gone about their daily lives pursuing their dreams and sticking to a disciplined financial plan. Every one of these everyday people miraculously have a common denominator. . . they all understood thrift and the power of compounding that thrift over decades.

Whether it is by using coupons or after-Christmas sales, these smart consumers continued their disciplined approach as they marched towards financial independence. Sounds easy, right? Not so, with the constant media hype from social, print and television sources, spending is overtaking thrift for many consumers. A well-organized financial life entails a prudent balance between savings and spending.

However, when human desires factor into the equation, being thrifty seems to take a back seat. Elementary desires and passion for the "latest and greatest" conspire to "spend now" – instead of "storing up" future purchasing power. Is that just how we are wired? Behavioral scientists could prove that point and advertisers seem to know what buttons to push. These multiple wants tend to have a positive effect on economic progress…good or bad depending on your viewpoint. Today's wants become tomorrow's needs and the cycle continues to go around and around.

So, when and how does one get off this not-so-merry-go-round of the constant battle between "needs" and "wants"? If it's too late for the baby boomers, then "teach your children well." Credit Graham Nash, and sung by Crosby, Stills & Nash with these lyrics……

You, who are on the road must have a code that you can live by.
And so become yourself because the past is just a good bye.
Teach your children well, their fathers' hell did slowly go by.
And feed them on your dreams, the one they fix, the one you'll know by.
Don't you ever ask them why, if they told you, you would cry,
So just look at them and sigh and know they love you.

And you, of the tender years can't know the fears that your elders grew by,
And so please help them with your youth, they seek the truth before they can die.
Teach your parents well, their children's hell will slowly go by.
And feed them on your dreams, the one they fix, the one you'll know by.
Don't you ever ask them why, if they told you, you would cry,
So just look at them and sigh and know they love you.

Just a classic song, perhaps about life's financial lessons.

Here are some ideas leading to being thrifty at fifty. . . and beyond.

First: Maximize your retirement savings to finance your retirement

48

years. Remember the human machine eventually wears out. A portion of the annual production should be set aside each and every year. Set this goal of becoming thrifty (needs vs wants) and stick to it. (e.g., IRA's, 401(k)'s, etc.)

Second: Establish an emergency fund to take care of life's unexpected events. Also, set aside funds to provide for life insurance, disability and health insurance (whether personally owned or employer provided).

Third: Establish an investment portfolio to help provide educational needs for children or travel, if desired.

Fourth: Conspire to be your own CEO. Create a side fund, to fund your entrepreneurial desires. Thrift leads to opportunities for self-reliance, which in turn can lead to the development of one's own enterprise.

Fifth: Consider the necessary steps to keep together what you've spent a lifetime putting together. Prudent estate planning, including wills, trusts, health care proxies and durable powers of attorney are tools the thrifty use to preserve their assets.

Every individual has the capacity to save, albeit at different levels. Saving and being thrifty merely means storing up the reserves instead of continually exhausting purchasing power. One has to defer the wants in life to the appropriate time. Transform your mindset by transferring present desires into future stakes of satisfaction. The result? A blank check for subsequent use in the future.

This is not easy to accomplish because we are in fact just human beings. However, those with imagination, discipline and economic intelligence may forgo immediate gratification (wants) for the expectation of a later life of happiness and gratification. The Merriam-Webster Dictionary's very definition of thrift.... careful use of money, so that it is not wasted.... is the exact opposite of a spendthrift.....one who spends money in an extravagant, irresponsible way.

Changing one's paradigm can result in feeling thrifty at fifty . . . and beyond. Join the challenge, increase your intellectual capital and obtain that elusive Peace of Mind.

Time to Exit?

One common theme amongst newly retired people is, 'What do I do now?' Life is a journey, and retirement is a destination. Here are some pointers to keep in mind…. which will lead to Peace of Mind.

Securing your retirement income should be the first item on the agenda. The paradigm shift goes from accumulation to distribution. Take an inventory of your assets and absolutely prepare a budget. Remember, this budget should be flexible, mainly because retirement really evolves in three phases. First are the "go-go" years, where you are healthy enough to travel whenever and wherever you want. Larger dollar outlays are usually attached to these years. Next are the "slow-go" years, where you still have the desire to go, however the machinery now has some limitations. Your health is not as robust as it used to be, and as a result, your travel agenda becomes redefined. Fewer dollars are needed during this phase of retirement. The final phase of retirement is the "no-go" years. Here we have severe limitations, confinement, physically or mentally, and perhaps the need for ongoing care. As a result, dollars used for travel are now shifted towards financing the "no-go" years.

However, the circle of life still continues. How can we turn our attitudes towards old age from a defeat to a triumph? Time to let go and advance the next generation of business people. We go from being thrifty, building our nest egg, to the realization that our old machine needs new components, new blood. A paradigm shift, if you will, on our mental attitudes. Isn't it time to face our new reality?

What is our purpose in life? The desire to "broaden our horizons" should be an antidote to the fear of old age. Try something new; it just may be that simple. Remember life is more than just making money and accumulating material things. Life is much more than those things, and those who miss this truth, miss great joy and the satisfaction that comes into one's life from being of service to others less fortunate than themselves.

Old age can be a period of great wisdom and reflection. It can be an opportunity to pass on that wisdom and the accumulated experience to the younger generation. Pay it forward, if you will – been there, done that!

Be open to new ideas during your senior years and commit yourself with the desire of unselfish service to others. Remember, life is a journey and retirement is a destination.

Live, laugh, and love along the way, and return the goodwill. What better way to obtain Peace of Mind!

About Joel

Joel N. Greenberg helps clients obtain "Peace of Mind." Having a career in the financial services field, Joel's main objective is to help his clients "keep together what they have spent their lifetime putting together." Joel has been "securing generational wealth" since 1978, the year of his initial entry into his profession.

Joel's long-time career is a result of his ever-present philosophy of lending a helping hand. Being people oriented, Joel has been fortunate to build a lasting relationship with his clients, as they move along life's journey. Many clients in fact become friends, a bond that continues for many years. Trust, integrity and honesty are all adjectives that describe Joel, and as a result, his clients constantly check in and ask for his input on a wide range of issues, not just financial ones. Joel sees his role as a facilitator, mentor and provider. His "high touch" method of client contact is an old school approach in today's world of high tech contact. In this fast-paced world, his clients truly appreciate receiving a hand-written note or telephone call from him versus the impersonal email or text. His ongoing "thrill of the hunt" continues to motivate Joel's passion for his profession.

Having graduated from the University of Connecticut in 1975, Joel's initial foray into interacting with the public was his opening of a small retail bookstore in his hometown. Having built a successful retail operation, Joel then sold the business and entered the financial services field in 1978. His continued drive to help people allowed him to establish his boutique company, Wealth Advisory Services, LLC. The company byline "Securing Generational Wealth Since 1978" is more meaningful and relevant today than ever before.

Joel has helped educate and empower numerous retirees and near retirees throughout his entire career. His knowledge on wealth accumulation, wealth preservation and wealth distribution strategies has been highly sought after for over 38 years.

A featured speaker at numerous seminars, Joel has shared the stage with his network of other professionals, leading to the most important endgame for the client: "Peace of Mind."

You can connect with Joel anytime at:
- Joel@wasllc.net

At the office: (508) 756-6100
Toll-free: 1.877.WEALTH.8

Or on his cell: (508) 889-6334

CHAPTER 6

SET GOALS, GET MOTIVATED, MAKE SACRIFICES

BY BOB CHITRATHORN

Let's call them Brandon and Laura. We met when they were three months away from their wedding day. Brandon had been extremely motivated to organize the household finances. Laura wasn't as nerdy as Brandon when it came to the budget, but they communicated well and were on the same page. They were debt-free. They'd made a few missteps along the way. Just 32 years old, Brandon was embarrassed when we first met because he had liquidated a 401(k) to help pay off his last bit of credit card and student loan debt.

"But what the hell? At least we were able to do the debt-free scream on the *Dave Ramsey Show*," Brandon said.

Finally, that private school tuition and medical bill would be out of their lives forever. They paid some IRS penalties for an early withdrawal, but soon they had enough saved up for a $30,000 wedding: one where their best friend could sing, where his grandmother could slow dance with him, and where they'd say "I do."

I've never met another couple more on the same page as Brandon and Laura. To this day, they're still the easiest people to work with. There's something to be said about knowing what you want in life. And they always know. Everyone has that friend who takes an hour to decide between Pizza Hut and Dominos. Brandon knew before you even asked. When Brandon and Laura first came to me, their goals were detailed and organized. They wanted to sell their home and buy a bigger property in two years. Can we do it? Should we do it? Should we wait and save up enough to pay cash for a home or have a mortgage? They also wanted to put away as much as they could for retirement in tax-free investments, but also get tax write-offs when necessary.

After the wedding, Brandon called me one night and asked about the impact of selling his rental home out of state. We spoke of his bachelor party, the wedding and honeymoon, and of their big news. Laura was pregnant. "We haven't told anyone yet, but I wanted you to know that we need to make some adjustments to the finances for a few months. We're just praying for a healthy baby and we want to save up in case there's any complications."

We reduced their monthly contributions and once again began saving for the next big life event. Two months later, I was lying in bed watching a 'Friends' re-run when Brandon's email buzzes my phone.

Hey Bob,
We're going to have to stop our contributions entirely for a few months due to the fact that Laura had a miscarriage. We'll let you know when we're going to be ready to start back up again.
Brandon.

In recent years, we had productive planning meetings for their finances and we had even gone to a couple concerts together. The annual fee I was charging them to manage their assets wasn't a focus. What we had built was a friendship.

I'm saddened, but honored, to have shared that moment with them. Days later, during our review appointment, Laura and Brandon showed me photos from one of their friend's baby shower. Within days, Brandon's grandmother – who he had danced with at the wedding – passed away unexpectedly. The bouquet I sent to their doorstep couldn't make up for the hardships they were going through.

Having watched Laura and Brandon experience the loss of their child, I gained so much more perspective in knowing my impact in their lives. Aside from their parents and closest relatives, no one else knew the secret they shared with me. Laura's seven-month pregnant friend might not have beamed so bright in those pictures, had she known what her best friend was going through at her baby shower.

If there's a lesson Brandon and Laura can teach us, it's that no matter how planned or structured your life is, there's always going to be a curveball. But when you've planned well, when you've communicated, when you've talked through your goals, no setback is permanent.

Brandon and Laura have continued to make great decisions and were able to upgrade their house as planned. Their systematic approach to their finances is a characteristic I've found to be common among those who follow the wisdom of Dave Ramsey, who I have built many of my financial philosophies around.

If you think Brandon and Laura are a bit strange when it comes to their financial habits, you're right. The average 32-year-old in America isn't paying cash for a wedding or communicating openly about big, medium and small purchases. We're a consumer society that has evolved to focus more on 'I want' and 'I need' instead of paying attention to our basic responsibilities as mothers, fathers and financial stewards.

A father's funeral shouldn't be financed by a collection plate of generous donations. A child's education doesn't magically get paid for overnight. A retirement isn't just a vacation that you arrive at. In life and in your finances, being successful takes work and it takes a series of great decisions. It takes wisdom. It takes planning.

Everyone's goals are different and no two plans are going to be identical. But if I were to encompass the number one goal that every financial success story shares, it's the goal to figure out, "Can I do what I want to do and when can I do it?"

My clients hire me because I'm willing to make their day, and even if I have to, hurt their feelings. Your financial coach shouldn't be there to tell you what you want to hear, or to try to put you to sleep with commentary on how the next election and some volatile third world country's economy are going to affect your savings in the next few months.

If you're over the age of 50 and your average meeting with your investment counselor is spent reviewing statements and listening to a sales pitch, you're doing it all wrong. My philosophies are simple. I believe that a financial coach needs to be independent and unbiased. If any of your investment or insurance policies share the same name as your financial coach's organization, it's time to evaluate if what you're investing in is what makes the most sense for you.

In every client relationship, I imagine that we're both sitting on a chair. A one-legged chair is going to be less stable than a two, three or four-legged chair.

The first leg deals with education. Education is the willingness to know what it takes to do better. How do your investments work? How are you paying your advisor? If I took social security at 62 instead of 66, what's the impact of that decision? Take the time to make your finances a priority. An honest and good-hearted financial coach will patiently educate you on your options and ensure that your understanding of their recommendations is more important than his or her paycheck. Too often, I find that those who have made mistakes along the way, often did so because they were pressured into making a decision that they really didn't have enough information on. Find someone who has the heart of a teacher and who is willing to simplify what many others may convey as extremely complex.

The second leg is all about comfort. Education leads to comfort. My clients need to be comfortable with me, comfortable with my assistant, with my recommendations, and with their own personal finances. No matter what their situation is, they have to be ready to take charge, because taking charge makes them feel more comfortable. It can start with being offered refreshments and sitting in a relaxed, yet professional setting. Comfort is also excitedly answering the phone when your advisor calls, rather than pressing ignore for months on end. If you're dodging your advisor, are you really comfortable with that person navigating your financial future with you?

The third leg is confidence. Confidence stems from feeling educated and comfortable. My clients need to know that I'm leading them to a destination they see approaching, but don't know how to navigate. Like a GPS guiding you through a town you've never been, you have to trust that the device is going to get you to the destination you envision. Just like a GPS, your financial plan needs to be updated regularly as shortcuts and road closures pose a threat to you getting to your destination on time or early. Confidence in finance comes from knowing what your current situation dictates, and knowing that the steps you're taking are going to lead to a better life for your family and a better financial future.

The last leg that keeps the chair from teetering is value. You need to know how and how much your financial coach is compensated. If you've never had a conversation with your advisor about compensation, well you should. Give him or her a call, don't wait. This is one of the first conversations I have with my prospective clients, because both client and advisor should have clear expectations for the relationship. How am I supposed to provide someone great value, if I don't even know what they're looking for, how much they've paid in the past, or how much service they need from me? Too often, advisors are selling and telling, rather than seeking to find the right fit. For example, some of my clients need to talk to me once a month for their planning needs. And they pay me accordingly. Others only need to hear from me every so often to feel fulfilled. When your expectations are on the table from the onset, it's much easier to provide valuable service.

I'm always up front when it comes to my compensation. Our relationship is a two-way street and it's important for everyone involved to be confident, comfortable and educated about the fees involved in hiring a coach, so that you can truly evaluate the value of your financial professional. If you hired a personal trainer in hopes of getting chiseled abs and nice shoulder definition, you should expect that with your full effort and participation, that the coach should lead you to your dream body in a reasonable amount of time. You wouldn't expect to see that dream body in weeks, just as you shouldn't expect to see your finances turned around in an afternoon. A personal trainer will teach great habits and form that will lead to fitness over the long term. You should expect the same discipline from your financial coach. Does your retirement savings plan look sexy in the mirror? If not, get back to work. I, for one, know that a six pack is easier to get at a liquor store than it is at the gym.

Just as the gym can seem tedious, we also have to realize that it may take three years to pay off a credit card or it may take five more years to get to that dream retirement. But where you'll find the most value when it comes to financial advice, is working with someone who will not just open an account with you, but who will take the time to map out the destination and help provide navigation instructions along the way.

Ultimately, if we don't have all four legs on the ground, our relationship needs work.

THREE BASIC HABITS OF SUCCESSFUL FINANCIAL STEWARDS

1. Goals:
 Success doesn't happen by accident. Your future accomplishments need to be mapped out and they need to be measurable. Sit down and list out a few financial goals. This starts and ends with communicating with your spouse and financial advisor. I often feel like a part-time couples' therapist, because I've seen a handful of arguments when discussing goals. Work through it. It's important to not just discuss these goals, but to have these conversations in front of and with your advisor. In order for your advisor to fully understand you and what you want to accomplish, they need to be privy to deep conversations you have as a couple.

2. Motivation:
Successful financial stewards are motivated by their goals and motivated to learn. Those who make fantastic decisions over a lifetime do so because they're driven to understand what it takes to get themselves to the end goal. You need to make sure your financial goals are motivating and can move you.

3. Sacrifice:
Do I take the family to Europe or make that retirement account contribution? How about taking the family on a simpler vacation a little closer to home AND making the retirement contribution? In the future, your kids will appreciate not having to house you in their guest bedroom. They'll appreciate your helping them pay for their wedding. They'll appreciate you having all the time in the world to vacation with your grandkids (their kids) while you're in your 60s.

Sometimes sacrifices are beneficial in more than one way. Not only can you take your grandkids on vacation, but you've also taught your own kids how to behave like adults with their money. Sacrifice also works for you! Don't forget to live along the way. Too often, folks tend to save for a day that they never see. Find balance in your planning and your advisor should help you make today, tomorrow, and thirty years from now a happy financial day.

Acknowledgement:
Special thanks to my friend Ian Massey for helping me put this together.

About Bob

Suthipong Robert Chitrathorn (Bob for short), came from humble beginnings. Born to parents Puttachart and Sakul Chitrathorn, Bob was raised in a mobile home park in Colton, CA. His parents migrated to Michigan from Bangkok, Thailand in 1974, before settling in Southern California. Over the years, Bob witnessed the different lifestyles that people lived and of the possibilities that lay ahead.

To the Chitrathorns, life in America was a gift and they were proud. They worked hard to put food on the table and to put Bob and his younger sister, Crystal, through school. Bob was frugal as a child and would be happy having bread with nothing but cheese on it, but he was blessed nonetheless. He learned that perspective made all the difference in life.

In his mother's words, "Education is money in the bank." She still teaches nurses to this day, and with Sakul, a factory worker, both sacrificed to make a better life for Bob and Crystal. They paid for both kids to go through private grade school and high school.

Their dedication and sacrifice didn't go to waste. Bob received a scholarship for his first year at La Sierra University, before transferring to Cal State San Bernardino. He received his B.S. in Finance, as well as a B.S. in Real Estate, while minoring in Business Administration. Despite the rigorous course load, Bob graduated *magna cum laude* and was named part of the Golden Key Honor Society.

In 2004, Bob became a financial advisor, he wanted to help people make good financial decisions. Economics and finance always came easy to Bob. When his professors at CSUSB had to miss class, Bob would be asked to teach his classmates and answer their questions. He was recruited by many different financial firms before settling at the firm he knew was best for him. It was a firm that cared more about clients than themselves. Here he learned the importance of planning, and would later end up becoming Vice President of Investments and then on to Senior Partner.

With 12 years of industry experience, Bob has helped hundreds of clients reach their financial goals. Bob recently joined a newly established independent financial firm to help grow a new brand and to help shape the next generation of financial advisors. He holds the Series 6, Series 7, Series 63, Series 65 and life, health and long-term care insurance licenses. Bob has been married to the love of his life, Brittany, for three years. They live in their California home with their rescue dog, Mazy, a pool, putting green, and a Pittsburgh Steelers-themed bar that's perfect for Sunday Night Football.

If you're looking for Bob at 6:30 or 7:00 p.m. on a weeknight, more often than not, he's prepping for a case or still making phone calls to clients. His parents' work habits weren't lost on him, and he's usually the one in the office at the end of the night setting the alarm and turning off the lights.

You can connect with Bob at:
- bob.chitrathorn@planwithprovidence.com

CHAPTER 7

THE MULTIPLYING MISSION:
DR. BILL DORFMAN'S LAUNCHING PAD

BY JW DICKS & NICK NANTON

In our new book, Mission-Driven Business, we spend a few chapters profiling entrepreneurs that we believe exemplify timeless success principles. In this chapter, we'd like to share our interview with Dr. Bill Dorfman and his own personal "Success Manifesto."

If you don't know Dr. Dorfman, he's a reality TV star. A best-selling author. A wildly successful entrepreneur. A generous charitable contributor. A mentor to hundreds of kids.

And, oh yeah, he's a dentist.

Sometimes, a Mission-Driven business isn't about a specific purpose or mandate; sometimes it's just about the owner's proactive mindset and his determination to make the most of every opportunity that comes his way. As you're about to see, Dr. Dorfman always had a purpose to his actions, even as a young child – and, just as importantly, was always willing to go above and beyond what was required to fulfill his personal and professional missions.

That meant not simply building a successful dental practice that would serve his patients at the highest level - it meant using that practice as a launching pad to expand his personal brand into all forms of media, pursue entrepreneurial ventures and also provide mentorship and resources to those in need of them. In other words, Dorfman set and achieved multiple missions throughout his career that set him apart from the pack.

Dr. Dorfman had a modest upbringing in the San Fernando Valley area of Los Angeles. He received his undergraduate degree from UCLA and was accepted to what he considers to be the best dental school in the country, the University of the Pacific (now known as Dugoni School of Dentistry) in San Francisco. When he graduated from their accelerated three-year program, he was ready to go to work – but not in the traditional kind of hometown practice most new dentists start out with. Instead, his Mission-Driven mindset led him to go for something much different.

Having grown up with limited resources, I never really got to travel or see the world. I thought, if I graduate dental school and immediately set up a practice, I'll never get to see anything. So I heard about a clinic in Switzerland that hired foreign dentists – it was the only one in the world where you could work with an American license.

They had 400 applicants for this one spot, and there was no reason they should hire me – I didn't speak French, I had no experience, I was fresh out of dental school, I was probably the least desirable candidate. But where I may lack in some areas, I don't lack in persistence and tenacity. I called that director of the clinic every week for months, and I had every professor at my dental school write me a letter of recommendation. When there were ones who were reticent to write one, I said "I'll write it, you just personalize it."

The clinic director got inundated with all of these letters, but I still felt like I wouldn't get hired for the position. So I asked if I could take him to lunch. He said "You're in San Francisco," and I said "Doesn't matter, I'll fly out." A bold statement to make when you have no money. I literally took out a loan from my grandmother to buy a ticket, and I flew to Switzerland, where he ended up hiring me. I got the job because I wasn't just a piece of paper like the other 399 candidates. Instead, I was a person right there in front of him who seemed capable and eager – so he said, "All right, I'll give you a chance."

I stayed in Lausanne, Switzerland for two years, and it was an amazing experience. I still have close friends from there. One honored me not only by asking me to be best man at his wedding, but also the godfather to his son.

In 1985, Dr. Dorfman returned to the Los Angeles area after his Switzerland stay and opened his own offices both in Century City and in the San Fernando Valley, where he had grown up. When the Century City practice took off, he closed the valley offices and focused his energies there. After working there for a while, he was approached by Stanley Vogel, who had been branded in *People* magazine as the "Dentist to the Stars." Dorfman began helping out at Vogel's practice and the experience led to a significant turning point in his career.

I remember the first day I was in his offices, I saw Flip Wilson, Senator John Tunney and Linda Evans. I never met anybody like that growing up in the valley. What I ended up learning from Stanley was probably the most valuable lesson of all, and it wasn't about clinical dentistry – it was purely about how to talk to people, how to better communicate and how, especially, to deal with people in entertainment – this was a whole new breed to me.

I worked for Stanley for two years, and he gave me a very difficult case – I won't mention the person's name, but this was one of the most famous people in the music industry ever. He had a lot of dental problems, and I literally worked on this man for two years. I reconstructed his entire mouth with implants and crowns, and at the end of two years of treatment, on his last visit, Dr. Vogel walked in so he could see what I had done. Well, the man stood up from the dental chair, hugged Dr. Vogel and said, "Stanley, thank you, thank you, thank you."

I'm like, "Hello?"

The man continued talking to Dr. Vogel. "Oh, your associate is good too, but Stanley, thank you." I'm sitting here, thinking to myself, "Stanley didn't do anything." At that point I decided, "I am going to open my own business."

At the time, I was dating a young woman who worked at Triad Artists, a talent agency which was later bought out by William Morris. She introduced me to all her friends who worked in the mailroom – many of whom became agency executives. They helped me build my practice by sending me their celebrity clients.

Again, Dorfman's ongoing mission was never going to be limited to his practice. In 1989, he started a company he named Discus Dental, and its first product was *The Smile Guide,* a book designed to help people see how their teeth – and their smiles – could be improved by cosmetic dentistry. But it was a chance encounter that really took Discus Dental to a whole new level of success the following year.

I've always been very philanthropic. I was working out in the gym, and a woman named Cynthia Hearn, who was kind of an accountant to the stars, approached me and said, "Would you like to help raise money for children's cancer research?" I said, "Absolutely." She said, "You're a dentist, right?" I said "Yes." "And single?" I said, "Yes... but...." I wasn't sure where this was going. "Well," she said, "we're doing a bachelor auction and we'd like you to go up on the block."

There ended up being 15 of us men up for auction by 850 women. They lined us up by age and I was the second-youngest one. The youngest one, the guy behind me, was someone named Robert Hayman. Robert was the son of Fred Hayman, who owned and developed Giorgio Cosmetics – so Robert had learned a lot about marketing and product development. Robert and I became best friends overnight.

In 1990, there was this proliferation of all these whitening products. I thought it was a good business to get into, so I approached Robert and we developed a product called NiteWhite. NiteWhite quickly became the number one take-home teeth whitening product in the country. We were competing with some really big companies in dentistry, but we were a lot nimbler – literally only two people in the decision-making process – so we could easily navigate through problems and quickly come up with solutions.

We did something that had never been done in dentistry. Cigarette companies had figured it out early – make smoking sexy. It may kill you, but you're going to look really sexy doing it. No one had used sex appeal in dentistry; we did. Instead of using our wife or our sister's best friend, we hired real models – like "whoa, really?" beautiful, beautiful models – and we shot them naked. You didn't see breasts, but we shot it very clean like a cosmetic ad. We also made it multi-ethnic – all of our ads looked like a Benetton Ad.

If you looked at all the whitening products prior to us, they looked like a medical mishmash. We packaged ours beautifully – it looked like an elegant cosmetic in a box. We also flavored it and did a few other things that nobody else did, and we priced it affordably. And we hired amazing sales reps.

The company started to grow and grow and grow. In the first year, we did $2 million in sales. The second year $4 million. Then $8 million, then $16 million. Then I went back to school. I knew how to be a dentist, but I didn't know business – so I went to UCLA and I took night classes in business and accounting, things I needed to know so that when I sat in our board meetings, I could make a difference.

Dr. Dorfman was determined to make a difference in other ways too – and the success of his NiteWhite product allowed him to make his first substantial foray into philanthropy. Greg Anderson, representing a group of dentists that called themselves the Crown Council which was dedicated to promoting oral health and doing charitable work in communities, approached Dorfman and his partner with a proposal.

They wanted to know if they could buy our whitening product at cost – one of their members, Dr. Jeff Gray from San Diego, had come up with an idea they called Smiles for Life. The idea was they would run a national ad campaign for patients to come and whiten their teeth at a reduced rate. But, instead of paying the dentist for the whitening treatment, they would be paying Smiles for Life, which would donate proceeds to children's charities.

When we heard what they were planning to do, we said that we'd give them the product for free. We donated all the whitening product, and to date they've raised over $35 million for children's charities. That was when we really started getting into a lot of philanthropic endeavors – for example, we also helped fund the Children's Dental Center of Greater Los Angeles, which provides quality oral health education and treatment services to needy kids and their caregivers. As our company grew, we gave millions and millions to these different charities.

Dr. Dorfman was anxious to continue growing as well as contributing. It was time to find a way to increase his public profile and potential. That way actually found him.

One of my patients had been a game show hostess for Howard Schultz, a TV producer who was trying to launch a new show on ABC called Extreme Makeover. In 2003, she had lunch with Howard and he told her about this show - she said "You need to meet my dentist." She also set him up with the plastic surgeon, Dr. Garth Fisher for the show – and Garth also said "You should meet my dentist." Of course, he was my patient too.

So I got a phone call from them asking if I would do the show. This was before reality TV had really taken off. I was a little reluctant, because I didn't know what I was getting into and how they were going to treat these patients. After I met with them, I really liked them – I felt like their hearts were in the right place. We went and we filmed the pilot for Extreme Makeover. It had huge numbers – ABC picked it up for the first season, I think 22 episodes.

Dr. Dorfman immediately saw the value of this kind of media exposure – and was willing to take a short-term loss in order to realize some substantial long-term gains.

Whereas Garth wanted to have a lot of other plastic surgeons on the show because he was afraid of being targeted, I didn't – I wanted to be the only dentist. My very first patient on the show needed 20 daVinci veneers – 10 upper and 10 lower – and at the time I was charging $1,500 per veneer. That added up to $30,000 worth of dental work.

I made a deal with them. I said "I'll do all the dentistry on this show for free as long as I'm the only dentist and you give my laboratory credit for everything they do, because the lab bill is expensive. Also, I want to use the whitening product from my company." They said fine. I was virtually the only dentist on the show until it got so busy that I brought a few of my friends in to help.

Well, because of Extreme Makeover, our company just literally exploded. In that first year, 2004, our sales went from $76 million to $101 million. Then we went to $135 million the next year. We had our biggest year in 2007 – the last year of the show – when we did $176 million in sales. ABC didn't pay me, but I did okay.

With the proceeds, Dorfman was anxious to take on his next mission –

and this one would not be for profit.

The Crown Council had a boot camp program which was designed to teach skills dentists need to be successful in terms of running a practice from a business standpoint, nothing about clinical dentistry. Dentists would go through this program with their whole team and they'd say, "You know, I wish there was something like this for our kids." So the Crown Council founder created a mentorship program which was amazing – and they would call me in every year to talk with kids. I loved doing it.

Well, the Crown Council founder passed away at the age of 85 – and I really felt that left a void that needed to be filled. So I called his younger business partner, Steve Anderson, and Steve and I co-founded the nonprofit foundation LEAP, a motivational leadership program for high school and college students, aged 15-24. We teach kids skills they need to be successful in life, such as time management, money management, interviewing skills, and how to write a resume. We also teach them things like dating and eating etiquette, how to write appreciation notes and thank people. We do a whole segment on drinking and driving, and I do a program called "100 Year Lifestyle," where I basically say "At your age, if you take care of yourself and you eat well and you exercise, you should be healthy at 100." 60% of the kids come on scholarship and they are underprivileged. These are kids that come from families that could never afford to send them to a program like this, and they're brilliant kids.

What Dorfman and his partner provide is a concrete way to help their students attain the kind of Mission-Driven mindset that helped him succeed in so many different ventures.

One of the first things we do at LEAP, during the very first hour when the kids are sitting there waiting, I say, "When you woke up this morning, whether you thought you did it or didn't think you did it, you put a number on your head from one to ten, one being the lowest and ten being the highest. That's how you think about yourself. So how many of you put a ten on your head this morning?" All my kids that have already gone through my program know to put up their hands.

Then I ask, "How many of you didn't put a ten on your head?" The rest of the kids in the audience sheepishly raise their hands. I look at them and say, "Who picked the number? Did you have to take a test? Did you have to qualify in any way shape or form?" The kids shake their heads. I say, "You picked the number. If you don't think of yourself as a ten, no one else will. Wipe that number off and put a ten on there." And, throughout the week, we tell them to not only think like a ten, but to surround themselves with friends that are tens, to walk like a ten, to talk like a ten, that's a big thing. There's one kid, Scott, every night, he sends me a text, he says, "Dr. Bill, you're a ten million." That's great feedback to receive.

There are kids that come into our program that have never been told by anyone that they are good at anything. They had no support structure, nothing, and now they are part of a community of kids that will care about them and listen to them. They've got friends, people that want to make them better and it's amazing what happens. It's unbelievable, I see it all the time. Parents will say, "What did you do?" Well, number one, I'm not their parent, that gives me a big advantage because you can't talk to your own kids the way someone else can talk to them. Number two, I bring in kids to talk to kids. That's powerful. I surround these kids with great mentors, leaders, and idealists. Birds of a feather flock together.

I lecture to adults and dentists, but if you can help a kid, you can help them for 90 years. If you help an adult, you get the back nine - most people aren't going to reach their maximum potential in their 70's and 80's. With kids, it's this blank palette. I watch these kids grow up, I watch them become doctors and dentists, whatever it is they end up doing, and I take so much joy and pride in it.

Dr. Dorfman is now semi-retired from dentistry. Although his practice is still going strong, he only does dentistry about 20 hours a week. He's also still very much in the media mix, appearing in a new TLC show entitled *Smile,* and also producing his own series, *The Dr. Bill Show,* in which he follows up on people he mentors to see if they succeed in their paths.

There's no question that Dorfman was born with his Mission-Driven mindset. It's been his greatest gift and that's why he wants to pass it on to a whole new generation.

I didn't think outside the box. I didn't even know there was a box. I did things that nobody else did. For better or for worse, I just did them.

I wake up every morning, I'm the happiest person you'll ever meet, I don't take anything for granted, I'm so appreciative of everything. My feeling is if we can't make this world better for having been here, what a waste. I've been so fortunate and anything I can do to make this world better or make other people's lives better, that's what I'm committed to.

And that's a great way to live your life!

About JW

JW Dicks, Esq., is a Wall Street Journal Best-Selling Author®, Emmy Award-Winning Producer, publisher, board member, and co-founder to organizations such as The National Academy of Best-Selling Authors®, and The National Association of Experts, Writers and Speakers®.

JW is the CEO of DNAgency and is a strategic business development consultant to both domestic and international clients. He has been quoted on business and financial topics in national media such as *USA Today, The Wall Street Journal, Newsweek, Forbes, CNBC.com,* and *Fortune Magazine Small Business.*

Considered a thought leader and curator of information, JW has more than forty-three published business and legal books to his credit and has co-authored with legends like Brian Tracy, Jack Canfield, Tom Hopkins, Dr. Nido Qubein, Dr. Ivan Misner, Dan Kennedy, and Mari Smith. He is the editor and publisher of the *Celebrity Expert Insider,* a monthly newsletter sent to experts worldwide as well as the Quarterly Magazine, *Global Impact Quarterly.*

JW is called the "Expert to the Experts" and has appeared on business television shows airing on ABC, NBC, CBS, and FOX affiliates around the country and co-produces and syndicates a line of franchised business television show such as, *Success Today, Wall Street Today, Hollywood Live,* and *Profiles of Success.* He has received an Emmy® Award as Executive Producer of the film, *Mi Casa Hogar.*

JW and his wife of forty-three years, Linda, have two daughters, three granddaughters, and two Yorkies. He is a sixth generation Floridian and splits his time between his home in Orlando and his beach house on Florida's west coast.

About Nick

An Emmy Award-Winning Director and Producer, Nick Nanton, Esq., is known as the Top Agent to Celebrity Experts around the world for his role in developing and marketing business and professional experts, through personal branding, media, marketing and PR. Nick is recognized as the nation's leading expert on personal branding as *Fast Company Magazine's* Expert Blogger on the subject and lectures regularly on the topic at major universities around the world. His book *Celebrity Branding You®*, while an easy and informative read, has also been used as a text book at the University level.

The CEO and Chief StoryTeller at The Dicks + Nanton Celebrity Branding Agency, an international agency with more than 1800 clients in 33 countries, Nick is an award-winning director, producer and songwriter who has worked on everything from large scale events to television shows with the likes of Steve Forbes, Brian Tracy, Jack Canfield (*The Secret*, creator of the *Chicken Soup for the Soul* Series), Michael E. Gerber, Tom Hopkins, Dan Kennedy and many more.

Nick is recognized as one of the top thought-leaders in the business world and has co-authored 30 best-selling books alongside Brian Tracy, Jack Canfield, Dan Kennedy, Dr. Ivan Misner (Founder of BNI), Jay Conrad Levinson (Author of the Guerrilla Marketing Series), SuperAgent Leigh Steinberg and many others, including the breakthrough hit *Celebrity Branding You!®*

Nick has led the marketing and PR campaigns that have driven more than 1000 authors to Best-Seller status. Nick has been seen in *USA Today, The Wall Street Journal, Newsweek, BusinessWeek, Inc. Magazine, The New York Times, Entrepreneur® Magazine, Forbes, FastCompany.com* and has appeared on ABC, NBC, CBS, and FOX television affiliates around the country, as well as on CNN, FOX News, CNBC, and MSNBC from coast to coast.

Nick is a member of the Florida Bar, holds a JD from the University of Florida Levin College Of Law, as well as a BSBA in Finance from the University of Florida's Warrington College of Business. Nick is a voting member of The National Academy of Recording Arts & Sciences (NARAS, Home to The GRAMMYs), a member of The National Academy of Television Arts & Sciences (Home to the Emmy Awards), co-founder of the National Academy of Best-Selling Authors, a 16-time Telly Award winner, and spends his spare time working with Young Life, Downtown Credo Orlando, Entrepreneurs International and rooting for the Florida Gators with his wife Kristina and their three children, Brock, Bowen and Addison.

Learn more at:
- www.NickNanton.com
- www.CelebrityBrandingAgency.com

CHAPTER 8

SUCCESS INCLUDES SUCCESSION

BY JAMES W. FRANK

SUCCESS IS VISION, STRUGGLE, AND YOU CHOOSE THE PRIZE

A dream is merely a picture in the mind's eye, the vision you have for your future. Thomas Watson of IBM was once asked how he decided to build IBM. He said that he envisioned it as complete and then set about developing that vision. I pictured my first manufacturing company in a building that I would design and construct, with me in my office. I then set about bringing that vision into reality.

It has been said that the greatest number of dreams lie unfulfilled in the cemeteries of the world. Ideas and pictures of the future you want to design are not the problem. Acting on those ideas is the first limiting factor. Dreams do not have an expiration date, except the one placed upon them by the dreamer. Look around you. Everything that you see started as an idea first. And most of those ideas were born out of frustration or necessity - the parents of invention.

The night I realized my first major company was going to have to be painfully wound down, I woke up about 3 o'clock in the morning in a cold sweat. One of those moments of having your back against the wall, wondering what the heck am I going to do. And immediately you know you have to get real serious, real fast. At that moment I had no clear vision of what the next business would be. But, I had a clear vision what it would NOT be. That clear idea still provided a goal, big enough, charged with enough emotion, to begin again. I then set about creating a business without employees, without borrowing money, without inventory, and unlimited in global growth. I had, in fact, started with an opposite idea.

What ideas do you have that you can stand behind and get serious about? How many times have you looked at something and thought, I wish someone would make or improve that item or process? And how many times have you later seen your great idea in a store window, or on television, or online, and thought; I had that idea a long time ago. All successful business owners I have known, have told me that their life changed when they decided to get serious.

Have you written your ideas down and the actions you are going to take? If it is not written, it is not so, is my mantra. I learned a method from Brian Tracy early in life, the twenty idea method. The first several actions to solving a problem will come easily. In order to get to twenty, you will have to combine ideas, as well as take an opposite idea and combine again. The best solution may be to do item eight without doing item fourteen. You will feel it in your gut when you have a solution with which to get started. I have yet to have it not work for anyone.

Once the vision is clear, phase two begins – the struggle. It is only after the struggle that the prize is obtained. Most entrepreneurs, myself included in the beginning, would like to skip right to the prize. It is as if instant gratification is just not fast enough. Everybody would rather have pleasing methods for getting the prize as well. The choice is: pleasing methods or pleasing results. As is always the case, there is a price to pay for any success, and it is paid in advance.

The good news is that the struggle can be reduced if one is willing to learn from the mistakes of others who have gone before. I often hear business owners say that they are self-made entrepreneurs. I have learned through the years, that particular euphemism means they made most of the mistakes themselves. It is like they are proud of having wasted their precarious lives doing the wrong thing twice, just to make sure it was wrong.

The cost of learning from the mistakes of others is incredibly less expensive than learning only from your own mistakes. If you are reading this book, you have taken a giant step in designing your own success. I have been a student of success for over half a century. I have read over a thousand books on personal and business development starting with, *How To Win Friends & Influence People.* At age eight, I learned, Success is getting what you want. Happiness is wanting what you get.

I have learned from thousands of hours of audio programs, watched educational and inspirational videos and asked for help and guidance at every turn. I have a board of advisors that don't even know I am gathering wisdom from them. Remember, you never G-E-T until you A-S-K. Learning is always ongoing and change is the only evidence of life. Just remember, if you see a turtle on a fence post, it did not get there by itself.

SUCCESS IS BOTH TIME AND MONEY

Why do you want success? What is it you want to achieve? I have learned that everything you desire will require either time or money, or both. Let me ask you, which is more important, Time or Money? My answer is both. Isn't that what most people want? . . . for tomorrow to be better than today and their family to be looked after? We need money in life, and the time to enjoy it.

If you had asked me when I was eighteen years old what I wanted my life to look like when I retired, here is what I would, and did say. . . Just give me the freedom to live, self-sufficiently by water, where I can enjoy nature and have time to read and gain more wisdom. Let me have some kind of residual income, where money is working for me, instead of me working for money. Let me earn an income while located anywhere in the world. Let me help people leave the woodpile a little higher than the way they found it. Let me use my isolated hideaway as a base in order to travel the globe at my leisure, never exploring the same place twice. I wanted both time and money even then!

Today, my home and retreat are on a gorgeous, secluded group of lakes in the country. Eagles, Osprey and Great Blue Herron inhabit my panorama. Everything I visualized at eighteen has been manifested into my life. This is no accident, and luck was not part of it. It took years of goal setting with repeated action plans.

The question is then, how do you develop your success plan to have both time and money? The first rule of succession planning is to work yourself out of a job. That requires a significant change in most people's thinking.

Eighty percent of the effort required to get ahead will be dependent on your ability to improve yourself. Realize that when you are trying to figure out what needs to change to succeed – look inside to You, Inc. Even if you draw a paycheck, you work for yourself. You can still offer your abilities to the highest bidder. More people are working remotely than ever before. The good news is that you always own your own business. The bad news is that you own your own business. You must hold your own feet to the fire and use discipline and will power to do the things other people will not do in order to succeed. If you want to achieve your time freedom, you will need to learn to turn responsibility over to others eventually.

With my first business, I did everything myself. I sold all-season greeting cards to neighbors at six years old, which was easier than asking my father for money. The card company provided a system, which when followed, resulted in achieving the goal of money in my pocket. I was the salesman, accounting office, purchasing, and president. I did it all, however, I liked the president part best!

As I started a manufacturing and wholesaling company to finance my way through university, it was not long before I needed some help. Trying to be "jack of all trades" meant "master of none." I just could not complete all the tasks that needed to be done and still reach the high marks needed for graduate school. I remember friends coming over on Friday night, or the weekend, and having fun with my roommates, while I put together product and orders in my bedroom company. Often, they would try desperately to coerce me into giving up for the night and join the party. Sometimes they would offer to help so that the job could be completed sooner. Then one day, one of my housemates decided that his university struggle was simply not worth the effort. Since he was available, and unemployed, I hired him to help out. Big mistake!

I made the first delegation mistake that most struggling entrepreneurs make. I had an employee without a job description. I had someone willing to help, but I was not prepared with a clear plan so that I could hire the best person for the job. Before long, I was not happy with the return on investment, and had an unhappy person working for me while living under the same roof. Needless to say, the strain was detrimental to the growth of the business.

I heard Brian Tracy explain once that after his first year in an early business, he was going backwards. He realized that by doing all the administrative activities himself, he had neglected the most important part of his business, sales. Being busy is not the same as being productive.

Whether you are a health professional who has created your own job, a website developer, or virtual assistant who works remotely, you will find the solutions to your biggest problems have a pulse. At some point, your biggest struggle will be delegation. Successful people have gotten to their level due to personal expertise or skill. That is what sets them apart. They set goals and achieve them. Successful individuals also tend to think, initially, that only they can properly perform a process. Learning to delegate and let go, is one of the marks of a superior leader of people. It is also one of the largest, career-advancing struggles you will have, in going from success to significance, with the time to enjoy it.

If you struggle, as many do, with relinquishing responsibility, learn to inspect what you expect. Give direction and then follow up. The clarity of thinking in advance will save you sleepless nights of grief. Two things are for certain; the people directing must first have a very clear idea what they want to accomplish and, the best person to hire for the job is the person who can provide the best return on the human resource investment.

Resist the temptation to delegate simply in order to insulate yourself. At one point in my manufacturing business, I created "middle management." I wanted a flat corporate profile, however, department directors needed help. I hired a responsible person to direct the warehouse. I gave him direction and goals. The second day on the job, he came to me and said, John doesn't have anything to do. What should I have John do? I gave him instructions for John. The next day, he came back to me and said, John finished that and doesn't have anything to do. What should I have John do? It instantly hit me that this guy was being paid over $40,000 per year and I was doing his work. I said, here is what to do. On your way out to your car, please have John report to my office. If I have to tell John what to do, somebody is redundant, and it is not me. As happens repeatedly in life, first the test, then the lesson.

SUCCESS IS TIME FREEDOM

Many people have a desire to get into business. Having once contracted with a bank, evaluating business requirements, I discovered that few business owners have even thought about how they are going to get out of business. Like everything in life, failing to plan is planning to fail. If you want money and the time to enjoy it, your mantra needs to be, "How do I get out of here?"

This is how I expected to complete my manufacturing career. I figured some white knight was going to ride through my front door. He would say, I have worked 70-90 hours per week the last twenty years, to accumulate the millions of dollars that I am willing to pay to you for your company, so that I can work the 70-90 hours per week that you have been working to keep it going and expanding. Oh, and here, you can ride off into the sunset on my horse.

What is your exit strategy from your job or business? Time and Now are all you have. Is your prize result that you will monitor online business activities while photographing from a hot air balloon over a Kenyan reserve? Is it being with kids or grandkids at Disney World, and when they want something special, you say, hey, money is no object? Is your prize having one of your best friends call and say they are going to be in France, Ecuador, Thailand or Hawaii, and you say, I have time. I will meet you there.

SUCCESS IS TAKE ACTION!

1. Write ten goals on paper right now! Write your goals in concrete and your plans in sand. I recently took what I call a 90-day adventure to determine where I wanted to go next with my life. I don't have five-year plans as much as short term adventures. I keep my mind open to opportunities that may, and will arrive. However, my goal remains the same.

2. Why are your goals critical to you? You must have a burning, emotional desire. What drives you? What evokes a passion in you? What do you get excited about? Write it down!

3. How are you going to achieve those results? What is the very next thing that needs to be accomplished today – your "Most Important Thing" (MIT). Do nothing else until that is complete.

4. Examine your results and compare to your reasons why, or values. If your values are being met, repeat the steps until each of your goals are accomplished. It will require repeated effort to obtain all the results needed to achieve both time and money. You will need to learn things. Remember, your best thinking got you where you are now, however, let me also remind you; your past is merely part of where you are going.

Success means you are always in life's checkout line. Make sure your end result is worth the price you are paying.

About James

James Wm. Frank has been an entrepreneur most of his life, having started out by selling all-occasion cards to neighbors at six years old. Being from the front edge of the baby-boomers (1948), James has over half-a-century of business wisdom. In addition to personal and family experience, he has invested tens of thousands of hours studying business and personal achievement. He has successfully applied business basics to launching over ten corporations in manufacturing, wholesaling, retailing, sales-training, transportation, business and personal development. James has developed many businesses on an international scale, as he has travelled to five continents and twenty-six countries. James continues to focus on helping people around the world start and develop their own business ideas.

Having achieved his childhood dream of having both time and money, James uses humor and inspiration to speak to younglings of all ages to reach for the stars, to not only make a difference in their own lives, but in the lives of others. James contends: "We all have an obligation to leave the woodpile a little higher than the way we found it, and everyone has a legacy and a story to be told."

Many baby-boomers are taking new directions in their lives as they discover renewed vigor in the face of living longer, healthier lives. A second career is becoming common and expected. If you have a new passion, James wants to hear about it.

Today, James operates his cloud businesses from wherever his laptop and cell can be connected. It is not just money, but an entire lifestyle of waking up and saying, I can't think of anything to worry about.

For more information on James Wm. Frank and his upcoming books, connect at:
- www.boomertozoomer.com
- www.jameswmfrank@boomertozoomer.com
- www.facebook.com/Boomer-to-Zoomer
- https://twitter.com/Boomer2Zoomer
- www.instagram.com/jameswmfrank/
- www.flipboard.com/@jasfrank/boomer-to-zoomer
- www.pinterest.com/jameswmf/

CHAPTER 9

A WONDERFUL ADVENTURE

BY PAGE OLSON

Twenty years from now you will be more disappointed by the things that you didn't do than by the ones you did do. So throw off the bowlines. Sail away from the safe harbor. Catch the trade winds in your sails. Explore. Dream. Discover.
~ Mark Twain

It was after dark in early June 1999. I was standing in the gravel parking area on the property we had recently purchased and just finished moving on to. I don't remember why I was outside. I just remember pausing in the calm and quiet, taking in the beautiful way the full moon produced a silver effect on the Cedar and Douglas Fir trees that bordered the north side of our property.

I refer to the just shy of four-acres we now lived on as "property" because the sale had been classified as "vacant land." You wouldn't know that looking around. There were two trailers each hooked up to electricity, their own septic system and running water from a working well situated west of the trailers. There was also a carport and at least seven other outbuildings of various sizes, and shapes scattered about the property. All of them in different states of repair from useable-but-needing-repair to unsafe and needing to be torn down. Lastly there was lots of junk including the bulldozed remains of the original homestead that had burned down years before.

How did we come to be here? Were we out of our minds? Were we really doing the right thing? Only time would tell. Thinking back, one short year prior we had had no thoughts of moving. This entire adventure began one evening as I was headed upstairs with the children for bed. I remember all of us talking as the children and I slowly moved towards the stairs. The staircase was open to the kitchen. Dad stopped at the edge of the kitchen, I was in the hallway between the stairs and the kitchen, our 5-year-old son was hanging on the end of the banister at the bottom of the stairs and our 3-year-old daughter was sitting on a stair part way up looking through the spindles. The only part of the conversation I remember was our son commenting he wished he lived somewhere where he could "dig holes and chop down trees." Our daughter added that she wished she lived where she could have "horses live with her."

Over the next few months as my husband and I discussed the idea of moving our family from a comfortable and convenient life to a life of uncertainty and inconvenience, I thought back to the stories I had been told about the sacrifice my grandparents had made for the sake of, what they believed would be, a better life for their children. They had been living comfortably and securely in an apartment above a movie theater when they felt they needed to change their living environment for the sake of their children. They purchased a large piece of wooded land a short distance outside the city limits, put up a tent on a tent platform and moved in – no running water, no electricity, and no plumbing. Over the years the tent grew to be the house in which I was raised. And I was privileged to play in the woods and the creek, build forts and treehouses, shoot archery on the archery terrace, grow food in a garden, and cook dinner over an open campfire.

Our children were now challenging us, by asking us if we would be willing to do something similar – take a risk, make a change that could benefit them in ways we would not know for years to come. Our move would not need to require a change of job, additional financial hardship, or a long distance move from where we presently lived, but it would involve inconvenience, sacrifice, and letting go of the dreams and desires of others in our extended family. Were we willing to do this?

There was sentimental value in the place where we were presently living as this residence had been my husband's parent's home. The large comfortable two-story home sat towards the middle of a large corner lot in an upscale neighborhood. A manicured front yard graced the neighborhood while a completely fenced backyard, considered to be "big," provided the children a safe place to play.

All that was history now. As I turned to the southwest, toward the trailer we had chosen to live in, ready to walk back inside I could not help but scan our property. Through all the junk, feelings of uncertainty, and challenges I knew were to come, I felt at peace.

Over the next five years, we cleaned-up the property, addressed each out building in turn, and built a house. Our son dug holes, learned how to use an axe, and our daughter's wish came true; horses came to live with us. Along the way the children continued to teach us how to become the parents they needed us to be. All we had to do was slow down, pay attention and listen.

There is a two-way circuit between parent and child.
Each is constantly sending messages and receiving replies.
The messages influence the replies, and the replies
in their turn touch off new messages.[1]

VALUE OF PERSONAL SPACE

Personal space is not just that space directly adjacent to your physical being, but it is also a space you are in control of. A space where you feel ownership. A space where you can place your things and no one will touch them without your permission. A space where you can go when you need some time to yourself to reflect, calm down or just get away.

Our children had individual rooms in the house we moved from. While they did not spend a lot of time in their rooms, when sleeping they often chose to sleep in the same room, it was still their room. When we moved into the trailer they were to share one large room. I did not think much about it. It would not take long for me to discover an unconscious underlying need that having two separate bedrooms meant personal space – a space to which they could claim ownership. There was this need to be able to declare "mine, you can't come in." Working with the children, the challenge was solved by hanging sheets to outline two

1. Stella Chess, M.D., Alexander Thomas, M.D. & Herbert G. Birch M.D., Ph.D., *Your Child Is A Person*, 1965

personal spaces that included their beds. They could choose to have the sheet walls open or closed - it was interesting to see that they usually kept the sheets open. To give themselves more "wall space" and places to hang things, they helped each other lace together two-foot by two-foot peg board squares. While these "walls" were only one square high it was all they needed to further visually designate the mutually agreed upon spaces while also providing "doors."

It was interesting to watch how the children used these spaces: "inviting each other over," using them for self-imposed quiet time, keeping items that mattered the most to them, and decorating with pictures and other items that were of personal interest. This space provided a place for their individual personalities to flourish while still fulfilling their core need of feeling connected to the family.

A NEED TO MOVE TO COMMUNICATE

The importance of being connected and staying connected to our children cannot be underestimated. At the heart of connection must be the desire to seek to understand through both verbal and non-verbal means of communication. Children do a majority of their communicating through their behaviors as they just do not yet possess the necessary vocabulary. Even as their vocabulary increases, they don't have the ability to express difficult feelings or unconscious innate ways of being.

Living in the old house, my son had already demonstrated he needed to move. I had already asked the question "Why can't my son sit still"? In searching for answers I discovered some children are high-drive, high-energy. They are most comfortable when in motion or busy. A secondary activity actually helps them be more mentally attentive. As a result, I allowed my son to stand to eat, fidget when I read, and have conversations while we did things side-by-side.

By the time we had moved to the property, he had started – on his own – to choose to sit and eat. Unintentionally, I found myself thinking he should also be able to sit to talk and be still when I read. That did not last for long. I quickly learned while he could now modify his behavior to sit to eat that did not mean his core temperament had changed, nor that he was developmentally ready or able to sit for other activities. Using opportunities our new environment provided, we continued to strengthen our connection through lively and interesting conversations while we enjoyed doing things together around the property such as: cleaning up, splitting wood and building or repairing different things. As for reading, he quietly enjoyed playing with Lego's on the floor near my chair while I read aloud.

WATCH ME

Part of being human is the struggle of wanting to be independent and yet desiring to feel connected; wanting to do things ourselves and yet needing help. This internal emotional conflict - needing dependence and yet desiring to be independent - is very frustrating especially for young children who still need help but so desperately want to "do it by themselves." There are times, for safety reasons, you as a parent, have to say no or need to correct the action. But what about all those other times.

By her choice, our daughter wore a lot of skirts and dresses in her younger years even after we moved to the property. One evening at dusk shortly after our move, our 4-year-old daughter, self-dressed in a dress and boots, had retrieved her "just-my-size" real hammer and climbed an "A" frame ladder to help her dad pound nails into the roof of the carport. After reminding her of safety rules, I stood quietly at the base of the ladder and waited for her to "be ready to be done." Once accomplishing what she wanted to she climbed down and moved on to another experience.

Taking risks is an important part of growing-up. When we don't step back and reassess what is really important, we risk unintentionally and unnecessarily hurting our child's ability to connect with themselves. Risk fuels their sense of accomplishment – we need to support it.

Along the way, I discovered parenting is a collaboration of many small successes happening all the time every day. True success is not as much a thing we accomplish as it is a feeling that flows from within when we feel accomplished. Every time a child asks us to "Look what I did," "Look what I can do," "Look what I discovered," "Look what I found," or asks us "Did you know…" they are sharing their little successes; a newly discovered understanding that puts them in touch with themselves and their environment. It takes tons of these little successes to help them grow in self-knowledge, self-assurance and self-esteem. If we are not careful, we unintentionally trample on their ability to connect with themselves, us, and the world around them. We need to remember their successes are not tied to our perspective, but to how they perceive what they can and do accomplish.

While I am not advocating families move, for us it challenged us to grow into the mentors our children were asking us to be. They sought our willingness to provide them a lifestyle in which they would thrive. In the end what our family has gained is much greater than what we lost.

Our children are young adults now. They continue to experience the feelings of success/accomplishment as a result of discovering and engaging in their own individual "happiness of pursuit." If you asked our children how would you describe your childhood, they would reply: "it was a wonderful adventure." For us, it was most likely the best parenting decision we ever made.

About Page

Page Olson has a passion for helping parents learn how to use child-led play as a way to facilitate understanding and connection between: the parent and child, the child with themselves, and the child with the world around them.

Page was raised in a home with no TV. Page, with her siblings, enjoyed countless hours of play, engaged in a variety of experiences, and actively explored many different ideas.

Outside the formal classroom, Page's love of learning and passion for helping others was easy to observe from an early age. Formal classroom learning was frustrating and full of failures. Even though Page studied hard, her test scores and other work never showed how much she actually knew. One of Page's college professors said that she was smart but that there was something wrong with her. Following this college experience, Page found work, eventually landing a job as a Medio-legal Investigator for a Medical Examiner, a job at which she excelled.

Page was graced with children and became a stay-at-home mom. Because she never really felt understood by anyone, her parenting style was to seek to understand first by asking questions beginning with "Why is..." or "Why does..." rather than questions beginning with "How do I..." or "What do I..." Seeking understanding by listening to behaviors, observing the children at child-led play, and offering a multitude of different experiences Page and her children developed close trusting relationships. This was how she knew what to do when her son struggled in preschool – remove him. In seeking to understand, Page discovered both her and her son's brains are wired differently. While their learning styles and strengths have differences, both fall under the "dyslexic label." This lead to an unexpected but very successful eclectic home-schooling journey.

Over the last two plus decades while raising her children, Page has worked with multiple families and children in a variety of different activities including: instructing at and writing interactive hands-on learning curriculum for a natural horsemanship school for kids; involvement in cub scouting from starting or helping to start three cub scout packs – one for which she received the District Award of Merit, planning and directing summer day camps, and training cub scout leaders. Since 2004, she has volunteered her time with a non-profit fire-based historical organization where she presently serves as president, helped start and staff a museum, put together a power-point presentation on the Great Seattle Fire, and is in her sixth year of coordinating a free public fire festival event. Over these years, parents often turned to Page for help with their children when they found themselves going through difficult times.

Many of the parents Page has come in contact with have commented, we love what you do with our children but we can't do what you do. To help parents learn how "to do what she does," Page founded Innovative Play for Kids LLC.

You can connect with Page at:
- website: www.page-olson.com
- www.facebook.com/Innovativeplayforkids
- www.twitter.com/pageolson2
- www.linkedin.com/in/pageolson

CHAPTER 10

MEASURING SUCCESS IN YOUR LIFE

BY JAYME HARRIS

Success is defined in many ways and means different things to all of us. Some people are after fame and fortune, others are driven and controlled by the need for power and to be "at the top." Success for others may be having a decent paying job, a nice house, and a loving family. Simply being happy is a great feat for most of us regardless of if we feel the need to be or already are considered a success by society or personal standards. For some, success is all of these things. What does success mean to you?

I used to be driven solely by the business world; having career success and making lots of money. It literally consumed me.

When I was a teenager I use to think that because I was totally poor and from a broken family, that I had it tougher than my friends. I didn't have money and nice clothes like the other kids, so how was I going to make something of my life with these kinds of obstacles?

We are given a perfect life . . . what we choose to do with it determines how far we can go and how many wonderful experiences we have. If we choose not to open doors and explore the unknown, these doors become permanently closed, and so do the incredible experiences waiting behind them. There are no excuses not to have a great life.

One of my favorite quotes on success, that I found in my early thirties while working abroad, is by Ralph Waldo Emerson:

To laugh often and much;
To win the respect of intelligent people and the affection of children;
To earn the appreciation of honest critics and endure the betrayal of false friends;
To appreciate beauty, to find the best in others;
To leave the world a bit better, whether by a healthy child, a garden patch or a redeemed social condition;
To know even one life has breathed easier because you have lived.
This is to have succeeded.

I engraved this quote on a wooden plaque and it always sat on my desk at work. I read it every day. I wanted to ensure that I accomplished in my lifetime each of these things in my personal and business life. I came to realize that success was more than just making a lot of money and moving up the "social ladder." What good is money if we are too stressed out to enjoy it? How can we say that we are successful if we don't spend enough time with our friends and family and enjoy real moments together? Like family dinners, walks in the park, playing games, and spending quality time with our children? Smelling the roses!

I was starting to earn the kind of dollar figures I had always dreamed of, but at the same time missing out on so many things in life in my 30s. This quote helped me get back on track for true success. It has been a special part of my life since I first read it. I use this quote in my goal setting for both business and in my personal life; in continuing to be successful and ensuring that I really experience all that life has to offer.

To laugh often and much... something that's important to practice daily. This makes people healthier and happier. When we live in anger, frustration and stress, it is a waste of time. I truly believe that being in those states of mind prevent us from reaching our goals and true potential in life. At the very least they slow us down and negatively affect our health.

This part of success, and to have succeeded, according to Mr. Emerson, is the easiest of all to practice. Some days, finding the humor in things can be more challenging than others. But if you make a concentrated effort daily to laugh, smile, and have that effect on others, you will find your day and life to be brighter. The ability to make others laugh is what I consider a great asset. You can bring laughter anywhere; to a business meeting, on a date, more oftentimes than not, you can turn a heated conversation around by introducing some humor.

To win the respect of intelligent people and the affection of children... Winning the respect of my superiors and elders was always important to me while I was in the US Air Force, and as I grew older working around the greatest business men and women around the world. If I had not learned this lesson and was unable to shine amongst my co-workers, and stand out as a leader to these great leaders, I would have never developed to take the role later in my career of General Manager and co-founder of what is now a billion-dollar company, then on to being a Vice President. To win the respect meant to let go of my ego, listen, learn and actually apply what I was taught by my mentors.

To win the affection of a child can be more of a challenge than that of adults. You can't fool a child. When my son and I lived in Dubai, I was searching for a part-time driver. I'd enrolled Dylan in daycare and I needed a safe and dependable driver since I was working full time as a single mother. There were two that came with excellent references, but as it turned out, I didn't have to make the choice. I could see a clear difference in the interaction between my son and each driver. This made the decision very easy. I did not choose, my son did.

To earn the appreciation of honest critics and endure the betrayal of false friends... This can be a tough one if you have ego problems, which most of us do, myself included. Ego without self- awareness can lead you down a bad path – or at least a bumpy road.

As to earning the appreciation of honest critics:

There are times when people criticize you that you feel are out of line or giving unwanted advice. I like to take up the challenge by earning their respect and talking the criticisms through. What is initially perceived as criticism could be meant as true concern, or coming from an insecure place in that person and by talking it out, you may actually end up helping someone.

For example, I've had countless people get into debates with me about the wars in the Middle East, one saying, "How could you be the kind of person that supports and who profits out of those situations?" Instead of taking his remarks as an attack, I told him that I understand, from his view, how he could think this solely from what is shown in the media.

I further explained that I was side-by-side with the soldiers in those war zones, risking my life right along with them, and that I was a big part of bringing them supplies and critical equipment for their missions. I explained how the soldiers would tell me stories of their experiences with meeting the local nationals in these war zones, and how they saw the human side of war. I'd hear about how much they related to the locals as ordinary people, just like their friends and family. A lot of the soldiers were involved in outreach programs with the local community; and regardless of the bad guys, and the reason we were at war, we could not change that.

What we can change is the social economic factors by creating local jobs, building relationships and bridging gaps between our cultures. I explained that when people started to get employed, paid, and were providing for their families, they stopped killing each other and kept from going to the side of the bad guys for jobs and support.

I'll never forget when that same guy came back to me the next day after previously only wanting to debate. He told me that he'd talked to his nephew who had served in Iraq and that everything I told him was true. He thanked me and apologized to me for any offense I took. I told him, "No offense taken," and that "it is hard to really know the facts unless you are there living it and experiencing it." I thanked him for having an open mind and seeing things from a different perspective. This kind of open communication is powerful. It has the ability to changes lives and the world.

As to enduring the betrayal of false friends... Ouch, this is a tough one! I can still feel some of the old pain of when I have felt betrayed by friends and loved ones. I'm sure we can all relate to this feeling. Ego can be the culprit behind these feelings of betrayal, and feelings that our friends were not real, but fakes. When we put a label on someone as "friend", we also put conditions on them. For example, most of us would not expect the same kind of loyalty, respect and connection with a total stranger as that of someone we elevate to "friend" status. The longer we stay "friends" with someone, the more we expect from them.

It seems rational to most of us that a friend of only a few months might not fully understand our sensitivity and insecurity levels as would a long-time friend. Family members are automatically considered in our lives to be held to the highest of loyalty and standards at all times. One wrong move and we lash out at them for any actions we consider as a betrayal. I think we can all agree that we sometimes make it impossible for people to live up to our unrealistic expectations.

It is never too late whether it has been 1 year or 10 years, to heal wounded relationships.

Another great piece of advice that I received is: "be careful of the toes that you step on today, as they can be connected to the butt you kiss tomorrow." Too many people and situations come full circle in life and what you thought were not real friends during heated blowouts, can and will be your best allies in the future.

To appreciate beauty, to find the best in others... This is so easy to do, yet we tend to be drawn in by finding any and all faults in people.

In appreciating beauty, aren't we all a little guilty of just driving by those mountains, trees, incredible God-made landscapes and nature without saying or even thinking about how incredible and beautiful they are? Even the flowers? We live in such a fast-paced world that we simply forget to appreciate the beauty in people and places, and finding the best instead of the worst in people and situations. Ralph Waldo Emerson saw the importance of incorporating this practice into our lives for a reason.

Seeing first-hand the devastation of war zones, families torn apart and killed in the blink of an eye, their lives forever changed by war and natural disasters. I have seen beauty in these situations of how resilient people are. Demonstrated by their unstoppable will and having to pull together and rebuild their lives and villages despite the most devastating of circumstances. How much better do most of us have it? We have the choice to rejoice and to appreciate the beauty and many blessings in our lives daily.

What is amazing in your yard? A special tree? I used to love looking at our beautiful oak trees while growing up in Florida. I loved smelling the fresh cut grass. Are you really soaking it all in? There is beauty in everything and in everyone. Yes, everything and everybody has their flaws, if that's what you choose to look for. But concentrating on beauty is the point of this message, and a daily exercise I challenge you to. See how much the positive energy level rises in you and those around you.

To leave the world a bit better, whether by a healthy child, a garden patch or a redeemed social condition... I'm really happy to be a mother and to have fulfilled this part of the quote. I'm also proud of being a Veteran of the US Air Force and subsequently serving over 15 years as a civilian contractor alongside the bravest of the brave of our U.S. Service members around the world – working side-by-side improving the social conditions of these local economies in war torn and developing countries.

If you have a child, grandchild, nieces, nephews or that special someone you have encouraged or mentored in life, Bravo! Everyone needs a person in their corner that they can count on to root for them when no one else seems to care or believe in them. Just being that person with a listening ear that can offer much needed encouragement really makes a huge difference in someone's life. You might never know the ever-expanding ripple effect that you have created. I had one person that totally believed in me and encouraged me to join the Air Force when I was 18 years of age. I was so doubtful and if that person would have discouraged me or was hesitant and not encouraging when I asked for their advice and support, no telling how my life would have turned out.

To know even one life has breathed easier because you have lived...

In reflecting back through my life with all of the ups and downs, successes and failures, I can see where my pursuit for knowledge, happiness and further developing myself has positively affected others, but more importantly, it has lit a clear path and passion for me to give back to others more than focusing on personal gain. I have a burning desire to help that kid or young adult with their pursuits in life. If I can pass on some of my knowledge and personal experiences of traveling to over 34 countries, starting a successful international company and gaining many unique life experiences with cultures from around the world to those eager to venture out into the world also, it gives me a sense of fulfillment and success in line with Emerson's quote.

I encourage you to use this quote to make your own life masterpiece and creation. Find practical ways that you can apply it to your life, and in turn experience the kind of success that money can never buy, and reaching the highest of heights of any social ladder can never fulfill.

About Jayme

Since 2001, Jayme Harris has worked internationally and is co-founder of Unity LSS, a billion dollar company focused on construction, manpower, logistics and supply chain management for the United States Government contract support throughout the Middle East and based in Dubai, UAE. She is the author of *Dare, Dream, Discover*, which was published and sold on Amazon and in American Borders bookstores. Jayme has been featured and interviewed on Fox News and KTLA TV.

Jayme is a world traveler, having worked in and visited 34 countries. She has currently relocated back to the USA and resides and works in Tampa, Florida. Established in 2016 as owner and founder of P&L Professionals, a woman and veteran-owned small business that services supply chain management contracts for the US Government. She is a military veteran and served in Desert Storm with the US Air Force. After an honorable discharge, she served for seven years as a Department of Defense employee at Eglin Air Force Base in Florida. Jayme is currently attending the University of Phoenix to complete her Bachelor of Science in Business Management.

Jayme simultaneously offers mentorship programs and life coaching with her sister company, I Consult Jayme. She can be reached at:
- iconsutljayme@gmail.com
- www.iconsultjayme.com

CHAPTER 11

DARE TO PROSPER

BY VICTOR EKE-SPIFF

Dare to Prosper is written in response to my passion over the years to give myself and my family a better life, and in the process, help others to grow and prosper. It is a dare, and very challenging but rewarding. I implore you to clearly set and relate with a right perspective for prosperity, so that your thoughts and actions can be guided towards a positive outcome. According to the late president of Bio-Lo Stores, Frank Outlaw:

Watch your thoughts, they become words. Watch your words, they become actions. Watch your actions, they become habits. Watch your habits, they become character. Watch your character, it becomes your destiny. ~ Frank Outlaw

Your destiny is the event or course of events that will inevitably happen in the future.

The Webster dictionary defines 'prosperity' as: "advance or gain in anything good and desirable; successful progress in any business or enterprise; attainment of the object desired..." It is God's heritage for us to prosper in life, so that we can grow and advance in every area of endeavor, and in a creative way, so that we can influence everyone that crosses our path positively. Although everyone of us is unique and different from all other human beings who have ever lived, the divine will of prosperity for all continues to act through our minds, heightening our desire to have more and more in every area of our life.

A complete life covers four common areas, namely: health, relationships, creative expression and financial freedom. On a scale of one to ten, with one being the least satisfactory and ten being the most satisfactory, you can do a quick assessment of your gain in each of these areas, by rating your results from one to ten.

- **Health:** Everyone desires to enjoy good health, both mental and physical. We all desire a sound mind, free from burdens of the past and anxiety of a 'would be' future. A sound mind is an active mind, a happy mind, consciously directed and engaged with activity of the moment. We all want to be physically healthy and fit, to be vibrant, zestful and energized every day, and to accomplish our tasks faster.

- **Love and Relationships:** All of us desire to enjoy excellent relationships – intimate, personal and social relationships – with people we love, like and respect, and who love, like and respect us in turn.

- **Creative Expression:** The drive for creative expression urges us to physically and socially manifest our unique talents, strengths and perspectives. More simply, you are who you are, and you are different from others because of the unique way you express yourself.

- **Financial Freedom:** The desire of all is to achieve financial freedom, to reach the point in life where our financial needs are adequately met and we never have to worry about financial lack again. For example, you want to be able to order dinner in a restaurant without using the menu pricing to determine what you want to eat.

The idea of prosperity speaks to us through our discontent and longing. Our discontent is the feeling of dissatisfaction over things or situations in particular area of our life, which lead to a desire and a longing for more and better things or situations in that particular area. The things we see and experience in each area are created in the mind, either by design or by default.

Hebrews 11: 3 states: *Because of our faith, we know that the world was made at God's command. We also know that what can be seen was made out of what cannot be seen.* In other words, everything in life is created twice, it starts with a thought in the mind, before it manifests in our life experience. Therefore, to experience prosperity in any area of your life, you must first conceive and nurture the idea of prosperity in your mind. It is the mind that evolves the idea of prosperity in the form of prosperous thoughts that become prosperous actions, . . . that form prosperous habits, . . . that form prosperous character . . . and eventually bring about a prosperous lifestyle.

The mind responds to two things: repetition and pictures. Repetition reprograms the mind to align with the intended actions that will bring about the desired outcome. Pictures are invisible images you see in your mind of the desired outcome. It is only what you see that you can achieve. Furthermore, the mind creates in two ways – by design and by default. If an idea is intentionally conceived in the mind, then it is by design; but if the mind picks a pattern from the past, then it is by default, which is unlikely to yield positive results.

Now, ask yourself, "Do you need positive mindset training?" I implore you to honestly respond based on the current results you are getting as you mentally sweep your mind over the four common areas of life. How is it going? And if your results are not exactly as you would like them to be, then you might, like the rest of us, need some positive mindset training. I, for one, absolutely do every day of my life, and have been feeding on mindset training for over 20 years now. So then, if you have misgivings in any of these areas, just note it as a discontent. And the score you like is your longing in that area.

I dared to prosper! I have benefited hugely over the years from positive mindset training and I love to teach it to others in many ways. I know that I am who I am today because of my strong desire to be be a better person. Why am I doing this? I am doing this because I want to enjoy peace and understand what happiness is. Now, I generate better clarity of purpose in every area of my life. I am more vibrant and energized starting my day, accomplishing my tasks and overcoming challenges. I generate more positive ways that express who I truly am, what I think, need, and desire in the world. I focus more on doing things that move me towards my dreams, and I enjoy increasing influence with my family, friends, and everyone needed to accomplish my goals.

WHY PEOPLE DON'T PROSPER

In the "parable of the sower" (also called parable of the soils) in Matt 13:3-9, Jesus tells us: *A farmer went out to sow his seed. As he was scattering the seed, some fell along the path, and the birds came and ate it up. Some fell on rocky places, where it did not have much soil. It sprang up quickly, because the soil was shallow. But when the sun came up, the plants were scorched, and they withered because they had no root. Other seed fell among thorns, which grew up and choked the plants. Still other seed fell on good soil, where it produced a crop – a hundred, sixty or thirty times what was sown. Whosoever has ears, let them hear.*

Learning from the parable of the sower, there are four kinds of people in the world, every one of them is characterized by a mindset and a corresponding set of habits and behaviors. God wills prosperity for everyone in the form of an idea, a dream or desire. He that is by "the pathway" receives it and throws it away in ignorance of his heritage, and continues to live in misery. He that is by "the rocky or stony ground" receives it with joy because he catches a glimpse of the way out but is too lazy to put forth the mental effort necessary to figure the way out and harness it, and soon abandons the idea for some supposedly juicy–looking, short-term alternatives, ruled by past events and people, and may live a seemingly comfortable life. He that is "among the thorns" receives it and because he is completely overwhelmed by too many unprofitable ventures, he gets stuck, confused and never decides on any one because of fear of failure. He that is by "the good ground" receives it, and understands his heritage of prosperity and works to accomplish and enjoy the fruits of prosperity.

The Bible says the seed of everything is inside of itself. Therefore, the seed of prosperity is inside prosperity, and God sows that seed in everyone so that we might grow and become his harvest. Yes, his harvest. Because that which is part of the whole is as well the whole in part. It is seed when you are sowing and it is harvest when you are reaping. Everyone is born a sower. That which you hold in your hand today is part of the last harvest, and it might just be the seed for you to sow today, so to guarantee for you the harvest for next season. Every sower sows with the end (the harvest or yield) in mind. By the laws of sowing and reaping, whatever you sow you will reap in multiplied form. As you sow the seed of prosperity, you are like a farmer scattering seed in a field. While you are about your business day by day, the seed keeps sprouting and growing, and you don't understand how. It is the ground that makes the seeds sprout and grow into plants that produce grains. Apostle Paul said, "I planted the seed, Apollos watered it, but God made it grow." Your mind is that fertile ground!

MY STORY

As a teenager, the way I saw prosperity was that it was all about money and the material things like clothes, cars, houses, jewelry and electronics, that money could buy. I also grew up to believe that I would have to work and study hard so I could get a good job and good pay, in order to acquire material possessions and prosper. I did study hard, and got a juicy job that actually afforded me with the material things my money could buy, but I still had a nudging feeling about something that was missing in my life, and the feeling grew stronger and more frequently by the day.

About seven years into my marriage, I was providing my family a great time financially, believing I was prosperous, and believing that was all there was to living. But it dawned on me one day, that I was losing that deep connection with my wife and children. I returned home from work one day, and my five-year-old son paid no attention to me at all, which was unusual. I tried to play with him but he wouldn't play with me. While I pondered over the unusual development, he further stunned me by asking, "Daddy, when are you going back to work?" I immediately sensed something was amiss. And one thing was certain, it was a wakeup call!

Ironically, before this time, I was already studying books and attending programs on personal development, and preaching it too, but I was still confused. I confided in my boss and mentor where I worked, and he said to me, "Victor, I trust you on the job. I trust you with your other colleagues here. I can say they all hold you high by the way you address issues and solve problems, all kinds of problems. You just need to be clear and focused on the area that is demanding your attention."

Eventually, I accepted responsibility for my ineptitude, renewed my perspective of prosperity, and I am still applying the principles in every aspect of my life. Prosperity is not all about money and the good things money can buy, as many people still think today, but prosperity is the value of mind that determines your achievements in every area of life.

Six Steps to Prosperity

1. **Describe your discontent and longing in any area of life, each with one word.**
   Tip: Both words usually are opposite in meaning.

2. **Test the word for your longing: Should that word be actualized in your experience, is it worthy of you? Does it enliven you? Does it fit your core values? Does it require that you grow? Will you need a greater understanding for that word to be actualized? Will it impact positively on others?**
   If the answer is yes to all six questions, then go to Step 4. If not, continue with Step 3.

3. **Refine your perspective of that word that describes your longing for a right intention, such that the word continues to align with the tests in Step 2 above.**

4. **What matters now is, "Why do I want it to happen?" and not "How can I make it happen?"**
   And for what you want, as you begin to relate with your "why" – which is your passion and the deep-driving desire – something extraordinary happens; as getting clear on your "why" puts you on the same feeling tone as what you want, and the connection begins to grant you access to the way out.

5. **Begin to voice what you want in gratitude, and assume the feeling of your desire already fulfilled.**
   Tip: Cultivate the use of positive statements relating to your desire and every other situation around you. Positive words become positive actions. Initially, your confession / statement might not sound convincing, but as you continuously repeat to yourself the positive statements, the sense of believing will come. As you continue in this way, you will begin to see the "How's" show up in your life: ideas, resources, people, opportunities, etc. will begin to answer to your need that will make your desire fulfilled.

6. **Caution! Whenever you seem to get stuck on the "how", as offences (fears and anxiety) will come, you can only overcome by just acknowledging them, and you rather intensify your affirmations and focus on the feeling of your desire already fulfilled; that is a way to insist on the "why".**

Stay open to solutions and opportunities. Listen for answers that may appear in the form of a conversation, an article, or piece of advice you hear from a friend, or colleague. You will be amazed at the results!

CONCLUSION

Many have read and studied the law of the mind, and it is allegorical to the law of the farm, but only a few truly understand and practice its principles. I am passionate about how to control thoughts and can help you achieve whatever you dream or desire. You achieve your dreams by first understanding everything is created twice. Before it became a thing, first it became a thought. What we hold in our mind eventually produces its kind in our life experience.

This is the ultimate in daring to prosper.

Do it not for your self alone, rather do it to help build up a community of prosperous people.

About Victor

Victor Eke-Spiff is a Speaker, Coach, and Trainer. He helps people to discover, develop and deploy their dream so that they can live a life of meaning and purpose.

For 35 years, Victor Eke-Spiff worked with Nigerian Agip Oil Company (NAOC) Ltd, joining the company as a Supervisor-Trainee, with a Diploma in Petroleum Processing Technology obtained from the Petroleum Training Institute (PTI). He rose through the ranks to senior management positions such as Health Safety and Environment (HSE) Manager and Quality Assurance Manager. He represented NAOC in the HSE and Security sub-committees of the Oil Producing Trade Section (OPTS) of Nigerian Chamber of Commerce, Mining and Industry; and served as the NAOC representative on the Board of Directors of Clean Nigeria Associate (CNA), a Company jointly owned by the major oil producers in Nigeria for Tier-2 Oil Spills Emergency Response.

Within these 35 years, he honed his leadership and managerial skills. He trained, coached and mentored hundreds of others, most of whom have become high-flyers themselves.

Due to his burning desire for personal development, he continues to participate in seminars, teachings, coaching and training programs of top motivational speakers and success coaches of our time, including: Brian Tracy, Bob Proctor, Mark Victor Hansen, Jim Rohn, Mary Morrissey, and Brendon Burchard, to name a few.

In 2015, he started his new career, following his passion and calling for helping people discover, develop, and deploy their dreams, thereby living a life of meaning and purpose. The Life Mastery Institute (LMI), a premiere coaching center for transformational coaching, certified him as a Dream Builder coach. He has been seen on stage with Mary Morrissey, CEO of LMI, and featured in *USA Today*.

Victor Eke-Spiff loves playing the piano. He and his beloved wife, Edibau, reside in Port-Harcourt, Nigeria, with their three sons and one daughter.

To contact Victor:
- Telephone: +234 806 949 6081
- Email: victorekespiff@yahoo.com
- Website: www.myvitorio.com

CHAPTER 12

DECIDE EVEN IN THE MIDST OF ADVERSITY

BY CHARLES KEY

Guilty was the plea I made. Standing in front of a judge agreeing to something I did not do to avoid something I did do. At no time in my life over the last 20 years, you would have had me believe that I would be standing here answering the question, "HOW DO YOU PLEAD?"

As I stood there, time stopped in my mind. I temporarily bought into this-is-the-end-of- life possibilities and a pity-me mindset. Right then and there I decided not to buy into it, and would use the anticipated slowed-down time to study, increase my knowledge, perfect a new craft and learn everything I could about all the thoughts that I had in my mind. I was determined to become more. Reality then kicked in as to where I was and time started again, and I entered my plea and began what many would say was the 'nail in the coffin' for any career. Was I starting another chapter in my life?

This journey began 20 years ago as a US Army Veteran of Desert Storm/ Desert Shield turned serial entrepreneur. My entrepreneurial journey ranged from my first brick and mortar businesses of a wheel and tire shop to a very successful decade-filled career in Real Estate – ranging from being an investor buying and selling over 250 houses, apartments, notes and numerous commercial and residential consultations, business educating, consulting and coaching upcoming entrepreneurs on business formation, business capital and credit and business operations. I owned teams in the American Basketball Association including the TEXAS

TYCOONS as well as serving as the VP of Marketing for the league. I formed an independent record label the Deep South Tycoons in which we earned an entry on The Billboard Top 100. I started a media company Crimson Multimedia, which owned a majority interest in different regional and national urban magazines. I even had a stint as a movie producer for six different independently-released films. A lot has been accomplished and experienced but none of these ventures prepared me for this pit stop in life.

After paying my two-year debt to society, I was told that a felony in my chosen profession was a dagger in the forwarding of my career. I told myself it was a stepping stone in life. I considered it a pass or fail lesson in internal fortitude. I sat down and wrote my goals down for the hundredth-plus time in my life. I decided to select a vehicle which would allow me to run as fast as I could while working on a legacy income strategy.

That vehicle became the Network Marketing and Direct Sales Industry. I knew several individuals with backgrounds from various walks of life, from the nefarious to Corporate CEOs, that had achieved different levels of success with this chosen path. The one thing I love about Network Marketing and Direct Sales is your past doesn't dictate your future, your desire to win does. I always knew that from the State Pen. to Penn State, from the Penitentiary to the Penthouse, Network Marketing doesn't care, just go win! I put my head down and got focused in a company I had previous experience with, but minimal success in.

I was determined to learn the skills to become a professional Network Marketer. I put on blinders and immersed myself in every multi-millionaire network marketer training I could locate, any material in any format. I worked with blinders on for 17 months after the 'pit stop', to earn one of highest positions in a multi-billion-dollar debt-free corporation. The consistent and persistent actions positioned myself and several of my team members to build the same level of income and more than had been afforded me over 20 years as a real estate and business consultant.

Through this journey, I have learned several valuable life lessons to live by.

I want to share 4 of those with you:

1. *The first lesson is to be aware of whom you are getting your advice from.*

   My thought pattern is that a person who is not where you aspire to be can never tell you how to go on a journey they have never personally been on themselves. I found, as I made my decision to pursue my goals, the best resources of guidance and information was from individuals that had achieved what I wanted in life, family, health, happiness and wealth. This quote sums it up: Beware of the naked man that offers you his shirt.

2. *The second lesson is you become what you put in your mind and focus on.*

   I learned that if you focus on the negatives of life you will attract more negatives. Your lack of action allows more negatives to accumulate, which intensifies your **bad** situation. You have a choice. You can focus on and grovel with negatives or you can **decide** to live, eat, and sleep your positives. These strong positive mindsets will manifest in your life through success-driven actions. Instead of seeing life thru a microscope, you start seeing the positives lights of potential through a kaleidoscope.

3. *The third lesson is position yourself around positive, ambitious, success seekers.*

   You will become the average of the five people you surround yourself with the most. I live by a code, *If I am the smartest person in the room, I am in the WRONG Room, it's time to go into another room so you can learn and grow.* The financial and mental resources in a room full of multi-millionaires and business owners will always be vaster than a room full of employee-minded individuals due to the experiences derived from life. In order to grow and become more, you must surround yourself with a better you. You must always be learning and growing your mind so that *you can be more, do more and have more!*

4. *The fourth lesson is know why you are trying to obtain success!*

   You must have a solid reason that moves you in order to succeed.

If your reason is money, when times get tough you may decide the fight is not worth it and convince yourself you will try something else. My **WHY** is my family. I decided I want to position my family to benefit from the generational wealth I decided to build through Network Marketing. I decided that it would be up to me to start building a legacy of prosperity and philanthropy.

Your WHY will change from time to time as you achieve your goals. It may start as your family, decreasing your debt, your retirement, college for your child or your grandchildren. Once achieved, then your priorities may change, and then you may decide you want to help hundreds, thousands or even millions to achieve their goals. You may decide to help heal a world issue you feel passionate about. Whatever your WHY is, it has to be a choice made where you will not give up just because the path gets a li'l tough.

Life's journey will always have its ups and downs. It boils down to how you react and what is your response. Will you lay down and say, woe is me? Will you let your circumstances of life dictate your success? Create your success through mentors, accountability partners, modeling, and continuing building who you are. Personal development will make you overcome all obstacles. Answer your calling to become what you were put on this earth for. Grow! Expand! SUCCEED!

About Charles

Charles Key is a U.S. Army veteran and a serial entrepreneur. Over the last two decades, Charles has been an active real estate investor in both commercial and residential. Charles also served as a CEO or Director of several organizations which he formed in various industries – including real estate investing, business consulting, credit and capital formation, sports management, an independent record label and entertainment production.

In the last ten years, Charles joined the network marketing/direct sales industry. After looking at several companies, Charles cast his lot with Stream Energy, a debt-free eleven-year-old company with over $8 billion in sales, operating in the United States in the Electric, Gas, Mobile and Home Protective services field. Charles was promoted to the prestigious position of Executive Director by Stream. He is building a massive team within Stream by leading by example, and through building, training, personal development and thoroughly promoting duplication.

Charles pours nearly 20 years of knowledge, experience and wisdom from working with thousands of individuals in all of the fields he has immersed himself in. Through turmoil and adversity, Charles Key stands tall and continues to help individuals achieve a higher goal. . . Freedom and a Stress-Free Life to Build a Legacy.

Connect with Charles at: www.successisnotfree.com

CHAPTER 13

INTROVERTS:
THE UNDERESTIMATED POWER

BY ANTJE BRUCHNER

"You always have a different view on things, that's why I come to you if I have a problem," was just one of the feedbacks I once received from a colleague at the end of a management course. I don't like feedback rounds. Hardly ever did anyone tell me something about myself of which I was not aware. But this specific comment kept me busy for a very long time, because I was wondering why my advice should be different from others. Did it not just reflect my thoughts and logical reasoning?

At the office, I noticed that I was the only one who could barely concentrate when people were talking or the radio was playing. Noise distracts me and after a day at work I am often very tired – am I a bit sensitive?

I avoid the limelight, feel alone in large groups, require plenty of private time to recharge my batteries, and tend to listen more than I speak. I am annoyed by people that are obsessed with constantly telling others what they do and have accomplished in their lives, and by people that ask questions in a meeting only to attract attention.

Huge parties, phone calls, or office meetings can easily become too much. I don't like small talk, but in one-on-one situations I start blooming, especially if I can talk about something in depth, and even with a bit of philosophizing. My boss thinks I am disinterested in his meetings because I'm not saying anything. In fact, I just don't want attention. I have understood the 'big' picture already, and I will say something only when I think it could be important.

People around me seem to see me as being different and polarizing. They like to party, don't overthink things, live and enjoy their lives to the fullest while asking me if I'm OK, only because I'm lost in my thoughts … again. I feel alone and misunderstood in my own world.

Literature deals solely with eccentric, successful and loud types of people, and helps them to rule the world even more. But by accident, two books fell into my hands, which deal with the opposite. And all of a sudden, I identified myself in there. I noticed that nothing is 'wrong' with me and that the problems I am confronted with are just common. I did an introvert 'test' and the result was that I could find in myself nearly every attribute of an introvert. Dealing with this helped me to understand who I am, why I am how I am, and why I sometimes feel so misunderstood.

I am relieved now to find that there are many of 'my kind', the ones that like to be on their own, like to think, to delve into more detail and don't like conflicts. But even more importantly, the 'quiet ones' are doing great and important things in this world and are really cool people!

However, I also noticed that it is important that one understands the other. That we understand that not only the thinking and behavior of men and women are different, but the same applies for different cultures, introverts and extroverts. Thinking about and reflecting on ourselves helps us to know and understand ourselves, our reactions and those of other people. It helps us understand and strengthen our potencies and to identify the hurdles.

In our society, there are many *well-known examples of INTROVERTS*. Surely, you find lots of introverts that are philosophers, innovators and scientists, as they need to be very persistent to be successful. What makes them successful is mainly one thing: they remained true to themselves with their introversion and all the other attributes that came with it. Joanne K. Rowling, Tommy Hilfiger, Woody Allen, Lance Armstrong, Frederic Chopin, Marie Curie, Charles Darwin, Clint Eastwood, Michael Jackson, Bill Gates, Albert Einstein, Michelle Pfeiffer, Steven Spielberg, Gabriele Strehle and Mark Zuckerberg are just some you can find in this famous group.

In *politics* we also find introverts. Barack Obama and Angela Merkel are widely seen as the strongest and most successful national leaders in the industrialized world. Undoubted are Barack Obama's oratory gifts, but as President he has also come across as quiet, scholarly and introverted – even stand-offish.

Angela Merkel is neither a natural orator nor an instinctive campaigner, though she has learnt to do both. But her preference, as Obama's, is to keep herself to herself. They each have a closely-guarded private life and a small circle of trusted friends. Angela Merkel has often been criticized for waiting too long until she finally makes a decision or takes a stand. But being calm and safety-oriented are typical signs of introverts, whereas extroverts are more reward-oriented and also more open for trouble.

Introverts and extroverts both have their own strengths and struggles, but introverts are the more underestimated. They are not a minority. The statistics you find indicate that between 25 and 50% of people are introverts. This means they aren't just controllers, researchers and IT specialists. But one thing is for sure, wherever they are they are at least as successful as the extroverts.

Most people, however, are not complete extroverts or introverts. Every person possesses introverted and extroverted characteristics, but are born with a so-called comfort zone, which is the general movement leeway and makes us more flexible. So if Barack Obama is giving a speech, this happens predominantly in an extrovert mode, which takes a lot more energy out of him than acting in the comfort zone. In getting older, people move more and more to the center between introversion and extroversion.

In recent years, *diversity* has become one of the biggest goals in international companies. Gender, religion, race, sexual orientation, etc., have all received their space and recognition in public life. However, the different needs of introverts and extroverts are unfortunately not yet taken into consideration. Considering that this is a crucial and important point in dealing with men and women, or different cultures, this will be an exciting development in the near future, e.g., in creating office spaces or setting up meetings.

The fact that the open plan is more and more taking over the office concept layout, creates a psychological strain for introverts. They need environments that fill their energy level, where they can concentrate and think, and where they can avoid being over-stimulated by other people and noises. Extroverts, however, love it, because they have the environment and perfect surroundings for brainstorming and discussions with their colleagues, which fill up their energy levels.

The Differences

Let's have a look at the main *differences* between introverts and extroverts, before exploring the positive sides of being a 'silent fellow.'

Being an introvert or extrovert is a total of how we were born, how and in what culture we grew up, and with what kind of situations we had to deal with. The central difference between introverts and extroverts can be seen in the way they are filling their energy levels. As mentioned in the previous chapter, the extrovert will find it in the exchange and interaction with others; the introvert, however, prefers having time alone to think things through before communicating.

Obviously, extroverts attract much more attention with their endless appetite for talk and attention, but they are not necessarily more effective. Extroverts dominate social life, so they tend to set expectations. In the extroverts' society, being outgoing is considered normal and therefore desirable, a mark of happiness, confidence and leadership. Extroverts are seen as bighearted, vibrant, warm and empathic.

Approximately 85% of all available (management) positions are filled with people that have a good relationship with decision makers. This creates a problem for introverts to climb the ladder in a big organization, as they don't like small talk, don't like to advertise themselves and might therefore just be overlooked. The skills of introverts, and what they are capable of achieving and offering, take a back seat in this world where the communication of extroverts dominates.

In 1921, when the psychoanalyst C. G. Jung dealt with both definitions, he didn't know yet that there are also significant differences in the brain of each. Introverts have more activity in the frontal cortex and in the front thalamus, where not only learning, thinking and problem solving take place, but also sorrows are residing. Brain research has also shown that introverts use generally much more energy with their brain activities than extroverts, and this excludes special mental challenges.

The biological difference between introverts and extroverts lies in the different forming of the autonomic nervous system – the sympathetic nervous system (extrovert) and parasympathetic nervous system (introvert). The brain tracks and the autonomic nervous system of an introvert are especially for concentration, learning, self-reflection and memory, whereas the extrovert is more focused on active action and external stimulation. With an understanding of these differences, we now focus on the strengths of introverts.

STRENGTHS OF INTROVERTS

For most of the time, introverts process impressions from what they see, think or experience. They spend a lot of time thinking about themselves or others, and about what should be and what is. This leads to very deep conversations with regards to different avenues and quality of thought. Introverts are generally more careful, which also prevents them from being judgmental. The introvert prefers a respectful distance when talking to other people. Only close friends will know what goes around in their heads and what is important for them and what is not.

Introverts are better listeners than extroverts and can also concentrate much better. They dig deeper into problems and life's mysteries, which is why they often come up with new ways of thinking and fresh and interesting perspectives.. Introverts don't like to talk about topics they are unsure or undecided on, and struggle making quick decisions on matters that have not been thoroughly thought through yet.

Introverts are normally quiet people with highly analytical and logical skills, which allows them to keep an overview even in difficult situations. Their inner peace creates clarity and a positive view on things around them. They are independent from the opinion of others and are not pleased easily. This makes it easier for them to do and say what they think is right and important. An extrovert needs feedback from other people.

The highest form of independence in introverts, however, is to take the focus off themselves. Their actions are not based on vanity, pride, ambition or craving for recognition; central to them is something substantial – like a project, other people or their needs. The ability for selflessness, however, can only be based on self-confidence. Independence therefore means autonomy and inner peace.

Introverts have a lot more empathy than extroverts. This allows them to recognize possible compromises much easier and they can mediate in a very diplomatic way, since they are not focused on any single interest. They have the gift of seeing various sides of an argument and therefore also consider ethical aspects.

Very often, introverts are talented writers and also prefer written exchange – including social networks - more than talking in person or via telephone. They prefer taking time to construct and put their thoughts on paper.

Introverts are also very persistent, which explains why there are many introverts who are scientists, as perseverance is an essential prerequisite for success! They like to challenge themselves (because with their focus on reflection and consideration, introverts are likely to be aware of their own weaknesses and limitations) and are reflective. Introverts are always prepared, can anticipate possible questions, challenges and obstacles and reassure those around them.

In professional relationships, people with a need to maintain their distance are often seen as inaccessible, less assertive, or even intellectually challenged. No need to say that this can be crucial for any career. However, in many situations, an introverted leader can be even more effective at inspiring productivity, innovation, and self-leadership than an extroverted one. Introverted leaders exude calm and consideration, and are simply cool.

The human species benefits from contrasts that complete themselves. Extroverts offer impulsiveness, spontaneity and motivation. Introverts provide clever pauses, deep relationships, reflection and an open ear.

It is well known that the most successful companies are family enterprises in which husband and wife share the management. The genius of the opposites seems to also apply for a combination of introvert and extrovert. The perfect example for the success of such a combination is Apple. Steve Jobs, as an extrovert, was a genius in marketing and a perfect communicator. He convinced customers and partners. This wouldn't have been worth a lot without Steve Wozniak, his initial partner, who was the one who created the devices.

CONCLUSION

Introverts may be common, but they are also among the most misunderstood and aggrieved groups in the world. Female introverts might suffer even a bit more and might be more likely perceived as withdrawn, haughty or timid. People often think that introverts are arrogant. I suppose this common misconception has to do with being more refined, more levelheaded, more independent, more reflective, and more sensitive than extroverts. Also, it is probably due to lack of small talk, a lack that extroverts often mistake for disdain.

It is important to understand that there is no right, wrong or obvious benefit in being more of the introvert or the extrovert. Both have their benefits and hurdles, even though being on the far edge of one side or other will invariably cause some problems for the individual. But understanding some of the most typical behaviors will help to deal with either yourself, with people that are like you or the opposite. It will help you to understand their special needs and to predict reactions to various situations and scenarios, and to use their respective benefits in the best way possible.

For the introvert, it is notable that being 'different' is not a disease It does not mean you are boring, lonely or disinterested. It is more about accepting it, using it as a strength, to do what is really important for you and to find your own 'species-appropriate' way of living.

We are most successful when we have identified our personality, take it as a given and make the best of it.

About Antje

Antje Bruchner was born in Germany. She was brought up in a family of engineers, but a product of Generation X, when computers took over a major role. At a young age, Antje started helping out in her father's civil engineering firm and after graduating from school, studied civil engineering. She joined a big DAX concern during her studies, and then she did her Master's in Facility Management, as well as Business Management for Engineers at the same time.

Climbing the ladder quickly in the Corporate Real Estate world, Antje went on a delegation to South Africa, where she stayed for three years, exploring the African way of working and living and extended her knowledge and experience in the whole life cycle of property management.

She immigrated in 2016 to focus on new professional challenges, writing another book and perhaps also starting her own business.

Understanding and getting to know new cultures and countries has become increasingly important for Antje, since she worked in various parts of the African continent. Based on this experience, it is not totally impossible, that there will follow another move to the United States, Australia or New Zealand in her years ahead.

You can connect with Antje at:
- antjebruchner@aol.com
- LinkedIn
- XING

CHAPTER 14

LEADERSHIP FUNDAMENTALS

BY JAY PERRY

A good portion of your success manifesto should be dedicated to leadership development – both your personal leadership and your organizational leadership. After all, if you are building your career, business, reputation or credibility, you need to be concerned with how you are perceived and most likely, what kind of legacy you will leave.

I think many times people buy into the "born leader" theory, wherein the idea of instinctive or inherited abilities, nature and natural abilities are given too much credit. I know it was true for me in my youth. It was promoted that there was a special class of people to which we didn't belong, only ones that were privileged with uncommon abilities were allowed such entitlements. The reality of abilities is that the vast majority of what we possess has been learned. The fact is that over 70% of what you have as expertise, was learned. Leadership skills are in the same class. Those skills are learnable by you and the people with whom you will surround yourself. So let's get learning those skills!

We will deal with some fundamentals and some advanced techniques in this chapter surrounding how you can gain a sterling reputation as an effective leader.

One of the fundamentals that you must tackle is the specifics of what you want to accomplish and how you are going to measure the success of that endeavour. Too many people use vague terms when they speak of the future they wish to create, and those vagaries will not lend anything to the manifestation of success. We all have the picture in our heads. It is absolutely vital that we bring that picture out and place it on paper. Specifics are what allow our minds to go to work to accomplish goals. For example, if you want more money, just how much money are you talking about? Write it down. If you have a new car as a goal, what kind of car is it? What options will it have? Where will you park it? I jest on that last one, but you get the idea. You must be specific in goal setting. Your mind will start to put the pieces together and once you realize the goal, you are able to be comfortable with the concept of success.

You can be as bold as you wish about these goals. I encourage you to go beyond what you think is reasonable as the end goal. Setting interim goals will help you stay on track but that is a different technique that we will talk about a bit later. When I started getting exposed to these tenets and started laying down my dream, it included a description of my lifestyle and how I would work. Just this year I fully realized one of those goals when I was able to carry on with my coaching practice remotely, working with my clients while being with my family in a foreign country halfway around the world from home. It was a specific goal I had set that I wanted the ability to travel and help people all over the world, at the same time spending quality time with those I love. The way I did the exercise was to build a scrapbook of the view from the future. I put together clippings of scenes that I wanted to portray for my vision, and now, a few years later, it is reality!

Once when giving a lecture at a conference, during Q&A I was asked what was the one thing great leaders had in common. My answer was humility. There are many styles of leadership that are effective and part of what I do is help clients identify which one will work best for them. However, if they do not have humility they will not be able to practice the most powerful leadership technique I have tripped over, listening. It takes humility to practice listening at what is commonly referred to as the Active Listening level.

Active listening is bringing all your focus to bear on the person speaking to you, to the point of being able to repeat or rephrase back to that individual what they just said to you. One of the challenges in practicing active listening is that the human mind (read Your mind) functions at thinking thoughts at about 400 words per minute. The average person speaks at about 120 words per minute. Do you see a potential problem?

Absolutely! The mind of the listener will wander. Humans have been conditioned to rapidly come up with the right answers, so what I commonly observe is listeners start thinking about what they are going to say to the speaker once it is their turn to talk. When their minds are busy, coming up with alternate lines of thought or solutions that they know this individual should take, they actually stop listening to the content and probably lose very important aspects of the conversation.

Active listening helps resolve that problem by forcing you into intensely rolling in your mind the words of the speaker and prepare to repeat or rephrase the thought back to them. I do it like this, "If I understand you correctly, you mean …" This works for me and it helps the person to whom I am listening to relax and feel acknowledged.

So thus far, we have covered that we can learn leadership skills and need to do so in order to build a successful position and legacy of which you can be proud. We have also discussed having very specific goals that will enable our minds to help us realize the plans we make. We want to maintain a humble attitude and practice active listening to the level of being able to repeat or rephrase back to the person speaking, just what they said to us.

We want now to turn our attention to another practice of good leadership that will be a keystone activity of yours while you work on fulfilling your success manifesto. This is followup. You will have so many projects, people, products or professional things on the go that you must develop a system of tracking and followup that becomes fail-proof. Did you know that when you followup with people not only do you reinforce the content of what you have discussed with them previously, but you also improve their perception of you as a leader? Two major advantages for the price of one! Keep people on track and improve your leadership image.

You will have to collaborate with others as you work toward accomplishing your goals. To that end, you must have this system that will keep you on track as well as those with whom you collaborate. It doesn't have to be complicated. It can be as simple as a spreadsheet or a notebook. For me my day-planner is key. I immediately put into my schedule the followup action on the appropriate date. If necessary, I will also schedule what I call 'touch-points' that will be check-ins with people to ensure they have not been sidetracked with what we agreed to get done. This communicates your serious attitude toward success and commitment to positive actions and getting results.

This is especially true of longer term projects that will require work over a period of time. It is easy for anyone, including ourselves, to get caught up with the day-to-day and be derailed off of even very important projects. Another aspect to guard against is the tendency to procrastinate. This may not be your downfall but do expect it of others. You can contribute to keeping them focused and progressing, as well as keeping yourself abreast of developments, and improve their perception of you as a leader all at once!

This is tied closely to interim goals. As previously mentioned at the beginning of this chapter, once you have a clear vision of what the end result looks like, you can break down the time marching toward you into smaller, more easily-handled chunks. It is something I expect you have seen before. If you have a 5-year goal and have done the exercise that puts the details together and the vision is clear, then break down the 5 years into 1-year increments. What will you need to accomplish this next 12 months, that will lay the foundation for the next 12 months?

So it goes like this; if your 5-year plan is to have a thriving company with a rainy-day fund of 6 months' worth of expenses banked, you need to obviously know that expense amount and divide it by 5 (the number of years to complete the goal). That is the amount that must be banked over the next 12 months. To further assist you in making this realistically achievable, break that amount into a monthly number by dividing the yearly amount by 12. If necessary, and dependent on your cashflow, you might want to look at the weekly amount. You see it all becomes much more manageable at this level. For example, my $100,000 rainy-day fund becomes a $385 weekly contribution to that special bank account ($100,000 / 5 years / 52 weeks).

Success is accomplished in small doses. It is very much like building a brick wall. You do not do it in one fell swoop. It is done one brick at a time. As each brick is carefully laid in place according to the plans, the wall takes shape as the architect pictured in her mind. I remember that from one of my earliest jobs. I worked construction for a masonry firm. Seeing the blueprints, distributing the materials in accordance with the formulas used to tell us how many bricks or blocks and how much mortar was needed, then it was the skill of the brick-layers to carefully put in place that particular piece of the huge structure that would be there on the building site shortly. Think of your strategic plans just like that overarching blueprint and your action plans as putting the individual bricks into the right place. Those are the interim plans you can make and check on easily, to see if they are accomplished and contributing to your success manifesto.

Another area that you will need to be sure to build is the development of those around you. It should be obvious that if you have employees you must be supplying the basics for them to be happy to stay with you and, more importantly, be engaged and committed to your success. Employees need several things but paramount is opportunity for growth and a supporting pathway to realize advancement. You, as the leader, must provide these things for them to prosper under you. Even in situations where it is not obvious such as business associates, be sure that you are being a "connector" for them. Be sure you are getting them closer for what they need for their personal success, even if it does not directly contribute to yours.

One of the leadership traits I found important is being able to share the leadership role. There is only one ultimate leader of course, but that ultimate leader recognizes others have abilities and are better suited to take the lead at various times. Look for aptitude and glimpses of leadership-ability in others, nurture (mentor) it, provide a clear path to develop it and allow that ability to be put to use inside your organization. Assessment can be a powerful tool in assisting you to identify and understand both yourself and your people better. Inside of my approach, assessment is the very first step we take with a client as there is always a component of self-awareness that can benefit all concerned.

Remember where we started this chapter in paragraph two, the untruth that there are "born leaders?" Leading yourself and your staff and even your customers and vendors is something you can do. You must practice, practice, practice the skill sets contained within this chapter. You can add this expertise to your list, so work at it, get some help (coaching, courses, reading) and embrace being a leader so you can fulfill your Success Manifesto!

Chapter Take-aways:

#1. Leadership skills can be and are, learned abilities.

#2. Be very specific in your goals and how you measure your success.

#3. Stay humble and practice Active Listening.

#4. Followup is a key attribute that will keep people on track and improve your leadership image.

#5. Procrastination is the downfall of many people and you can help manage it with touch points.

#6. Success is accomplished in small doses like a brick wall is built one brick at a time.

#7. Provide for others opportunity for growth and a supporting pathway to realize advancement.

#8. Look for aptitude and glimpses of leadership-ability in others, nurture and mentor it.

About Jay

Jay Perry was born in a small industrial city in Canada to a family of entrepreneurs in the automotive field. Working with the family business allowed him to learn the meaning of focus, hard work, efficiency and personalized customer service. Being in that environment also helped him figure out the nuances and challenges of small-to-medium sized enterprises (SMEs).

Before he was 30, he was running a multi-million dollar business in Toronto, Ontario.

He returned to school and graduated with a BSc in Psychology, which was instrumental in his work with other SMEs. Starting in 1990 he created a consultancy where he helps these SMEs figure out success strategies and systems in their particular business environments.

By focusing on efficiencies of process wherein Jay designs customized approaches to improving performance for his clients, he has helped and continues to help many of them to increase in size and scope and to become multi-million dollar firms in their own right.

It was clear, early on, that it was more than just the processes that needed to be adjusted within an established company. Jay discovered if the thinking of the leadership group was not likewise changed, those improvements would be short-lived and companies would revert back to old habits. This led to the establishment of the Leadership Development course that helps clients sustain improvements to their businesses by improving the leadership within their organizations. His clients range from $3 million to $300 million in annual sales, and between ten to hundreds of employees.

Now Ally Business Coaching helps both increase profitability and develop the abilities of leaders within client companies across North America.

Jay Perry is a regular columnist and source for business magazines writing on business process improvement and leadership development. Jay is a certified Birkman® consultant and habitually practices continuous improvement by constantly upgrading and invariably being the greatest help to his clients.

In addition to his corporate advisory, he has volunteered countless hours to his community and not-for-profits serving on boards of directors and advisory councils.

Jay currently resides in Toronto, Canada with his beautiful and talented wife, Kim and their wonder-dog, Katie. He has a grown daughter who is a successful lawyer in the Middle East.

His pastimes include reading, golf, movies and doting on their nieces, playing the part of the fun, crazy uncle.

He can discuss process improvement and leadership development by phone at: 416-587-1748, or email him at: jayperry@a-b-c-inc.com

CHAPTER 15

GET ENERGIZED, FOCUSED, AND DOWNRIGHT SEXY NOW

BY DR. KAREN LEGGETT

If you are a midlife woman, then you are probably a lot like me. Most likely you have spent most of your adult life caring for others. Without a second thought, you've handled keeping everyone fed, clean, comfortable and happy with undying devotion. You likely worked outside the home as well, pleasing your boss, the customers, and your colleagues. Do you ever wonder how you managed to seemingly float through those days with ease and grace, but now feel burdened, dragging to barely complete the most urgent tasks?

You may not be aware of this, but a large part of how you feel, and thus how you act, is controlled by a mix of hormones inside your body. The balance of these hormones plays a pivotal role in your ability to manage your busy life. And it is Estrogen, your main sex hormone, that drives your desire to raise families and care for others, even with a seemingly impossible schedule. However, as you enter your midlife years, hormonal changes occur and an array of signs and symptoms start creeping into your life that can be confusing and unattractive to yourself, not to mention others. You may actually be getting tired of "doing it all!" If you are, you're not alone – it's a perfectly normal feeling, simply based on your changing hormones!

Imbalanced hormones present in many ways! Hot flashes are just one of many symptoms and usually come late after your hormones have been imbalanced for years. In fact, some women never experience hot flashes at all. More commonly there are other changes you notice in life, such as barely getting through your day, let alone feeling energized enough to prepare a healthy meal. You might be gaining weight and feeling fat and uncomfortable. Your sleep may be interrupted with thoughts that seem to go on and on like a broken record. You hate feeling irritable, overwhelmed, and taking out your frustrations on people you care about. It's embarrassing to stumble with basic words when you express your thoughts. Sex can be the farthest thing from your mind, and you feel guilty about it. To top it off, you can't forget The Dry Vagina.

I am Dr. Karen Leggett, a board certified family and geriatric physician and fondly known as The Women's Midlife Specialist, practicing an integration of traditional and alternative medicine. I, too, am a midlife woman who has experienced the complete array of hormonal changes. Without ever resorting to prescribing horse-derived estrogens and synthetic progestins, I have helped thousands of women find connection and purpose within their changing bodies.

Given the opportunity, you would likely share stories full of emotion, describing exhaustion, frustration, feeling alone and misunderstood. You might say that you can't make sense of exactly why you feel dissatisfied and unappreciated. And deep down you may even fear you will grow old before you have been able to realize your dreams.

I knew I wanted to be a doctor since I was a little girl. And though my path has been far from smooth, helping women for the past 17 years seize both physical and lifestyle opportunities has been the greatest joy and success of my career. When you are in balance, you notice you are waking up with a smile on your face from a good night's sleep. You feel good about yourself and it shows as you confidently communicate clearly and succinctly. You're more organized and efficient, your work shines and opens up new opportunities to explore. You have more free time to exercise and eat better, and you love how you feel more attractive as your body responds to your efforts to lose unwanted pounds. Imagine having more time with your family and friends. Maybe even rediscover a hobby.

Through the decades, women who have used bioidentical hormones have enjoyed the physical benefits of balanced hormones far beyond controlling hot flashes. Balanced hormones can reduce the occurrences of heart palpitations, migraine headaches, urinary tract infections, mood swings, panic attacks, and insomnia. Balanced hormones can also help maintain a younger figure, and promote healthier, moister vaginal tissue, skin and hair, as well as reduce bone loss which helps prevent osteoporosis, debilitating bone fractures, poor posture, and back pain.

And there is more good news!

If you are not at high risk for breast cancer, you can balance your own hormones safely and effectively, with natural bioidentical hormones, available to you without a prescription!

AND

It is EASY to balance your own hormones!

To begin requires you to understand the basics of two major sex hormones – Estrogen and Progesterone. In this chapter I will teach you what you need to know, share with you my favorite natural bioidentical hormone products, and show you how to start using these products to benefit from balanced hormones right away!

If you are currently seeing an Anti-Aging specialist and use prescribed bioidentical hormones from a compounding pharmacy, I congratulate you! You already understand the importance of bioidentical hormones! Please read on to see if you are able to do it yourself and save thousands of dollars!

The two most common complaints women have at the earliest onset of hormonal change are insomnia and fatigue!

This is because the very first change that happens with your hormones is the decline of Progesterone, not Estrogen. Progesterone is your "calming" hormone that helps you sleep at night and stay calm during stressful times. The decline of Progesterone actually starts when you are 35 to 40 years old during a time called Premenopause, and has a profound effect on how you feel. Other common symptoms of declining Progesterone include mood swings, headaches, irritability, anxiety, depression, sugar cravings, irregular periods, bloating, breast tenderness, and bone loss. Progesterone also helps balance blood sugar by keeping stress cortisol levels in control. Stress and anxiety trigger the release of cortisol, which then stimulates the production and storage of fat, thus low Progesterone levels can promote weight gain. In addition, fatigue is commonly present!

Finally, Progesterone's balance with Estrogen is vital to healthy breast and uterine tissue. When Progesterone declines, an imbalance between Estrogen and Progesterone occurs, known as "Estrogen Dominance." It's not due to Estrogen increasing; rather, Estrogen Dominance is the result of declining Progesterone. As you can imagine, this one piece of information can potentially change your life by keeping Estrogen in check with its hormone-balancing partner, Progesterone.

If you start using bioidentical Progesterone in your Premenopause years, you will likely experience fewer symptoms when Menopause actually starts!

Following menopause, when your Estrogen levels decline, you may benefit from the addition of natural bioidentical Estrogens.

Estrogen supplementation during the first 7 years following Menopause does NOT increase your risk of breast cancer!

The belief that Estrogen increased a woman's risk of breast cancer is outdated. Through updated research, it has been determined that Estrogen does not increase the risk of breast cancer for up to seven years post-menopause, and that woman who took Estrogen during their menopausal years actually had reduced rates of breast cancer and experienced the benefits of stronger bone density! There is simply no research available to assess what happens after seven years.

The research is also clear that the best way to use hormones is in a topical form applied to the skin.

Your body actually makes three different types of Estrogens: E1, (Estrone); E2, (Estradiol); and E3, (Estriol). Part of each of these words is underlined to help you remember the differences. E1 has a "one" in its name so it is easy to remember. E1 = Estrone. E2 has a "di" in its name meaning "two." E2 = Estradiol. And E3 has a "tri" in its name, meaning "three." E3 = Estriol.

E1, Estrone, is the strongest Estrogen and is produced by fat cells after menopause and thus there is no reason to supplement with it. E2, Estradiol, is the most common Estrogen our ovaries produce before menopause and thus declines significantly after menopause and is most commonly supplemented after menopause. E2 is most helpful during the earliest years of menopause while your body is adjusting to lower Estrogen levels. E3, Estriol, is the weakest Estrogen and is most commonly used in combination with E2. E3 is also the most common form of Estrogen to use alone for vaginal dryness. And since E3 is the weakest Estrogen, it is the preferred Estrogen to use in the years beyond menopause.

Supplementing with bioidentical hormones is usually straight forward!

Reputable manufacturers of bioidentical hormones make standard doses of bioidentical hormones because the standard doses are usually just right for most women. Bioidentical hormones can be mixed and matched to find just the right dose for yourself depending on the severity of your symptoms and which stage of midlife change you are experiencing. I have two favorite bioidentical hormone companies which I most commonly recommend: Beizweiken and LifeFlo. Both are available on my website. LifeFlo products are available on other websites as well.

Use the following guidelines to start your hormone replacement.*
Always start with the lowest dose and do not use doses higher than recommended.*

Premenopause: Age 35 and up when you first recognize symptoms of low Progesterone

Progesterone: Start with 20 mg before bed on days 14 – 28 of your cycle. This can be increased up to 40mg before bed for symptom management and/or as you get closer to menopause.

Estrogens: none

Perimenopause: 2 – 5 years before Menopause, usually ages 47 – 53
Progesterone: 20 – 40mg before bed or divided twice daily for days 7 – 28 of your cycle. Higher doses are usually needed. *Progesterone must ALWAYS be used when supplementing with Estrogen.*

Estrogens: None if you are having monthly periods; E3 (Estriol): 0.25 – 0.5mg each a.m. if you are experiencing missed periods and/or hot flashes. Higher doses may be needed as you get closer to menopause. Use E3 on days 7 – 28 of your cycle.

Menopause: No Menses for 12 months – Average age is 52 years old (though it varies)

Progesterone: 20 – 40mg before bed or divided twice daily every day of the month. Higher doses commonly needed. *Progesterone must ALWAYS be used when supplementing with Estrogen.*

Estrogens choices:

1. None if Progesterone resolves menopausal symptoms and/or you prefer to not use Estrogen

2. E3 (Estriol) 0.25 – 1.0 mg every a.m. or divided twice daily

3. Combination of E3 and E2, Biest 50:50 or Biest 80:20; 0.5 – 1 mg each a.m. or divided twice daily every day of the month. You can use bioidentical hormones all month without cycling once you have gone through menopause.

For Vaginal Dryness during Perimenopause or Menopause

E3 (Estriol) 0.5 – 1 mg vaginally; start with 2 – 3 times weekly at bedtime for 2 – 3 weeks, then decrease to once weekly for 2 – 3 weeks and then once every other week as symptoms improve. Maintain weekly to every other week as needed for healthy vaginal tissue.

Applying bioidentical hormones to your skin is simple.

Apply your bioidentical hormones to different areas of your skin, alternating these areas every week to every other week. The best locations are ones lower in fat, such as your inner forearms, lower back, upper outer arms and shoulders. Inner thighs are also good if you are not heavy in that area. If you are using more than one hormone, you can apply them together or separately, it doesn't matter. The more cream you are using the more surface area you will need to apply the creams. Rub them in well and allow the cream to dry before putting on your clothes. It is best to apply your creams after you shower; however, if that is not possible, try not to shower for at least two hours after applying.

Important: Keep in mind It usually takes 2 – 3 months for your body to fully respond to your new treatment with bioidentical hormones.

For 17 years I have been treating hormonal imbalances in midlife women, and I can say with confidence that if you are like most of the women I have cared for, YOU can do it YOURSELF! I recommend that you learn more about assessing your personal needs, how to test your hormone levels, and how to adjust your doses through your midlife journey. With just the right amount of knowledge and guidance, you can experience the personal and physical health benefits of safe and effective bioidentical hormones throughout the stages of midlife. Imagine what all of this could really mean to you and your family!

If you would like to learn more about balancing your hormones, overcoming fatigue, and experiencing the full ripple effects of your own balance through midlife, I invite you to visit www.drkarenleggett.com.

Congratulations on protecting yourself and getting educated! Here's to Your Best Mid-Life Years Ever!

*The information in this book is not intended to replace your relationship with a qualified health care professional, and is not intended as medical advice. Dr. Leggett urges you to make informed decisions about your health, and to always check with your physician before starting or stopping medications or supplements.

About Dr. Leggett

Dr. Karen Leggett is a dedicated medical physician helping women thrive through the challenges of midlife and to feel healthier and happier while creating the lives they imagined as younger women. Dr. Leggett has always been a progressive thinker and strives to achieve a true integration of traditional and alternative medicine to help patients find the best treatment for themselves as individuals.

Dr. Leggett knew she wanted to become a physician since she was a young child. Her mother was her inspiration and guide to aspire to her dreams and mentor others. She also encouraged Dr. Leggett to go beyond the scope of traditional medicine and recognize the benefits of natural medicine, nutrition, and bioidentical hormones. In fact, Dr. Leggett's mother was one of the first women ever to use bioidentical hormones, more than 30 years ago and long before most physicians had ever heard of them. Her mother still serves as one of her greatest mentors, along with her father, ages 83 and 95.

Dr. Leggett's personal experiences have taught her to listen with sincere interest and communicate honestly. She has experience in many scopes of medicine, including practicing in the hospital, rehabilitation and nursing facilities, assisted living facilities, hospice, home visits, and office settings in both affluent cities and rural America. She has served on a hospital Board of Directors and been a member of two hospitals' Ethics Committees. Her experience goes far beyond the average physician, providing her a greater understanding of human nature which has helped her connect with compassion and understanding.

Dr. Leggett is a graduate of the University of Central Florida and the University of New England College of Osteopathic Medicine. She completed a residency in Family Medicine followed by a fellowship in Geriatrics. She has been attending conferences by the American Academy of Anti-Aging since 1999. She has been the President of Leggett Medical Group since 2004 and started the Women's Midlife Specialist practice in 2012, when she designed the "ABCs for Women" for training Nurse Practitioners in a year-long mentorship program she created to further expand her reach to midlife women. She has been on staff at Florida State Medical School and Lake Erie College of Osteopathic Medicine, and has given hundreds of lectures to physicians, physicians in training, nurse practitioners and to the public.

Today, Dr. Leggett is a leading physician in helping women balance their hormones, energize their lives, thrive with confidence, and overcome the challenges that are holding them back. Her goal is to help any woman, anywhere, who is struggling with the changes of midlife, empowering them with knowledge, direction and support.

You can connect with Dr. Leggett at
- www.drkarenleggett.com
- www.twitter.com/AskDrLeggett
- www.facebook.com/AskDrLeggett

CHAPTER 16

PASSION TO PROFITS

BY JOHN BEZERRA

It's summer in the early 70's, I'm seven years old, my weekly trip to the big city (Bakersfield, CA) was a short drive from my home town of Delano, CA. I remember being so excited, I get to go to Toy Circus, the biggest toy store in the world (at least I thought so) walking through the aisles in kid heaven wanting every other thing I see – train sets, Hot Wheels, Lincoln Logs and GI Joes. And then I saw it, yes there it was, with a light shining from heaven above, the infamous Dill Pickle bicycle, in all its glory, lime green custom paint, banana seat, tassels, and racing stripes. I knew she would be mine, I would be the envy of every kid on the block! I did the first thing that popped into my head, that's right, I begged, when that failed I went to plan B – yep, I threw a tantrum. OK, after my backside stopped stinging from the whupping I got, I was let down and had to endure the long (35 min.) drive home.

The next day my grandfather took me into the barn and made the deal of the century with me. He said if I were to raise half the money for the bike, he would pay for the other half. I was excited beyond belief. I'm a hop, skip and a jump away from riding off into the sunset on my beauty. He then told me I could help around the barn, and he would pay me $0.50 per day cash money. My seven-year-old math skills go to work and I realize I will get my pride and joy sometime around my freshman year in college. Hmm, time for all out massive action, I ask my mom if I could do extra chores, I mowed the neighbor's lawn (and I'm allergic to grass) but I'm on a mission. Then I had the Idea-of-all-Ideas. The kids at school played marbles and were very fond of the large (boulders) and clear (puries). I knew I could get $0.50 each for these and a whole bag of 50 cost only $1.99.

My first encounter with profit margin! I'm on a roll, I feel like the King of the playground. I have something people want and I'm going to cash in on the market. This is the point in my life that I knew I wanted to be an entrepreneur!

As I transitioned into my teenage years, I found a love for sports, all sports – football, baseball, basketball. But what I really started to gravitate towards was the individual sports. I became involved in wrestling, and my love of bicycles naturally transitioned into BMX racing. I was able to maneuver my schedule around school and the only job I've ever had in my life which was a chain Grocery store (this made me realize I just cannot have a J.O.B.). Now, I do not think I was a 'natural athlete' but what I lacked in talent I made up for in hard work! I studied the greats, watched films and read Books. If I had the opportunity to meet a great athlete, I would take it. When it came to practice, I would show up early, stay late, practice on my days off, lay in bed and visualize victory.

I had a burning desire to be the best, I wanted to stand on the podium, on the very top above the amazing #1. I became very successful. I eventually became a national champion at both sports. As I aged, I outgrew the sports, at that point in time there was really no financial opportunity in my chosen sports. The one thing that I had acquired through the years of training was a fairly muscular physique, I saw an opportunity here, most of these athletes were late 20's into their 40's. I was around twenty years old when I went into the competitive bodybuilding arena. I followed my same game plan – watch, listen, learn, and outwork the other guys. A few years later, I won another national title in a third sport.

This was the perfect occupation for me, I could train clients and work my schedule to fit in my own training. I quickly realized the monetary rewards in competitive bodybuilding were not enough to support a family (at this time I'm married and have a beautiful daughter named Sasha). But personal training was really picking up, and again I went to work, I got every certification I could, went to seminars, conventions, watched the successful trainers around the gym, and eventually got my degree in Kinesiology. One day, a mutual friend said he knew a TV actor that wanted to get in better shape for his character, which was filmed on the beach, and the majority of times shirtless. This was right up my alley, weights, beach, yes please! This was the door I was looking for. I then got referral after referral, and I was busy making unthought of money. I've trained TV and movie stars, worked for six major studios and I even have been able to appear in 4 movies and 3 TV shows. At the time of this writing, I'm co-starring in an Indie film.

Now let me clear something up please, this is not because I'm super human, nor do I have special gifts, and by no means call it luck. The funny thing is, the harder I work, the luckier I get! This is from one chance moment in a barn in Delano, CA, a seven-year-old had a vision, a vision of something seemingly out of reach, a vision that transitioned HIM into a world-class athlete and business man. You see, I had a gift that I took for granted, that was my Grandfather; yes, the very same one in the barn on that fateful day. I did not realize how amazing he was until I was older and wiser, and I never got to tell him how much he shaped my life. He passed away a few years back. This giant of a man was a man's man. If I could cast somebody to play him, I would probably pick Sam Elliot.

My Granddad John (my namesake) had an eighth grade education. This oldest of eleven helped support his family due to the deteriorating health of his father. Failure was never an option, He just had to make things work. As I grew up, I never heard the word 'can't.' He had a farm, a junkyard, a towing company, and a small trucking company, employing mostly his siblings. This is the true meaning of multiple streams of income. I can still hear him say you can do anything you want if you work hard enough – don't ever let anybody tell you otherwise.

Fast forward to modern times, a few years back, I'm now in my mid-forties. One day I woke up and realized my time is limited. I've been a successful trainer for now over 25 years, but to make the kind of money I desire, I still have to work 12 hour days/6 days a week, how long can I keep this pace up? I still have goals. Although the money is good, I could not say I had financial freedom, and I knew financial freedom brought another kind of freedom I have never experienced – TIME! I wanted time with my family. I wanted to make up lost time with my daughter Sasha, and now granddaughter Leah. The time was now or never, the economy was at an all-time low for my generation, so training, being a luxury, started to dwindle.

I kept hearing about these companies that allowed you to work from home, at your own pace. I saw a couple people I knew win trips, cars, and quit their long-time careers. I started asking questions and getting information online. The business was called multilevel marketing, or network marketing – Yep, one of those pyramid scams! Well, the deeper I looked into it, the more I realized that this was a legitimate business. I was blown away that the 'average joe' (no education, social circles or specialty knowledge whatsoever) could become a 6-figure or even 7-figure earner.

Another thing I found out was that more money is paid out in commissions than in pro sports, the TV and film industry or even real estate. WOW! Then the road block, I started researching companies, I just could not find one that I could be excited about. I would find a decent product but the compensation plan did not excite me, or it had a great comp plan but an inferior product. I have worked really hard on my reputation for years to get involved in something just for money. A couple years had passed and I had all but given up hope.

One day a friend asked me to come to his house to listen to a dear friend talk about a new company he is starting. He said it's in the health and wellness field and right up my alley. To be honest, I was not even a little interested, but he was a good friend and was really excited, so I went solely as a favor to him. I sat in the meeting with my arms crossed, I listened but with a very critical ear. He got to the comp plan and got my attention. Although not showing interest, I took the product samples, thanked them for their time, told them it's not really right for me, but the best of luck. Well, a funny thing happened, a few weeks later I tried the products and had probably the most productive day I've ever (yes, ever) had. I called my friend and said we need to meet right NOW, the world needs this. The rest is really history. I've got a couple cars, several vacations, top earner spot, and finally learned the power of residual income and the freedom and peace of mind that comes with it. Thank you, 1ViZN, for coming into my life at the right time.

Well that was how I got into network marketing, but how did I become successful? I think you can guess what I'm going to say next. I went to work, I applied the same techniques I have for everything I've done in my life. I studied books, online, interviewed people that have been successful, went to seminars, bought training tapes, etc. The company being new, had great training modules, but being new there were no 7-figure earners yet, I went outside the company and found a mentor, one being my co-author, Mr. Brian Tracy, among others. See, one of the best pieces of advice I can give a new person is, WHO DO YOU LISTEN TO? You must listen and learn from the people that have done it, the people that have the things and life you desire. But I'm going to give away the secret to all top earners or just successful people in general, ready? Its attitude, 100% attitude. If you have the right attitude, the facts do not matter.

AGAIN, IF YOU HAVE THE RIGHT ATTITUDE, FACTS DO NOT MATTER!

I'm going to finish this up by outlining my system to success. It is really just a list, a list of things I do on a daily basis. First and foremost, I start the day on a positive – I listen to an audio book or read for about 10-15 minutes. Second, I go out happy; try this, when you leave your house tomorrow, smile and say 'hello' to every person you come in contact with. This is a magical tool, you cannot be in a bad mood if you do this. When I meet people I ask them to tell me about themselves, I listen to what is important to them and I show genuine interest in them. I don't talk about myself nor do I try and sell them anything. People love to talk about themselves, and more importantly, they love feeling important – do this but be sincere, this alone will open more doors and provide more leads than you can handle.

Learn to love people and use money, do not get it turned around. My daily list is comprised of 5 items:

- Number 1 – Prospect XX people today
- Number 2 – Follow up with prospects
- Number 3 – Contact XX teammates today
- Number 4 – Do XX 3-way calls today
- Number 5 – Contact my loved ones and tell them how much I appreciate them

It's not hard, follow these steps and you cannot fail. Remember, have a big "Why" (why success is important to you), have a burning desire to succeed, make a game plan, create steps, write them down and do the work. Remember this is your business. Make business hours, do not let other things get in the way, and before bedtime your list has to have every item checked off.

SMILE AT THE WORLD AND THE WORLD WILL SMILE BACK.

About John

John Bezerra is an American athlete, entrepreneur and actor. He was born in the central California farm town of Delano. John began sports at a very young age, and played the typical team sports, but developed a love of individual sports, believing, "If I lose, there is nobody to blame but myself." Eventually, he became a national champion in three separate sports: Wrestling, BMX Racing and most recently, Bodybuilding. Earning a bachelor's degree in Kinesiology, John gravitated to personal fitness training, quickly establishing himself as the go-to authority in his area. His ability to change physiques safely and quickly gained him the attention from the entertainment world, and his resume of working with top Hollywood stars runs deep, and he still works with selected clients.

His entrepreneurial skills developed early. In kindergarten he learned that a $0.99 bag of marbles could net about $5 when sold individually, resulting in a visit to the Principal, at which time he was informed his mother did the same thing with cookies when she was in kindergarten. After building a Success Fitness career and profile, John kept hearing about network marketing businesses. After studying the business, attending meetings and listening to tapes, he learned the compensations plans. Meeting with million-dollar earners, etc., he finally found a product and system that worked with a compensation plan, and the resources to finally help thousands. Within months, John became the top earner in his company, and received the usual awards - cars, trips, etc. – but he felt the ultimate reward was to be able to change peoples' lives for the better, caring enough and showing people, no matter where they came from, they can have anything they desire.

John resides in Las Vegas, NV. He still trains select clients, has a thriving network marketing career and sits on the presidential board of his company. John loves public speaking on the topic of creating success; he's the former fitness expert on beauty you see on TV, and Vegas Life TV. John's been in a number of films, and can be recognized from seasons 2 through 4 on *Sons of Anarchy*.

CHAPTER 17

INCREASE YOUR SUCCESS WITH UNIVERSAL ENERGIES!

BY MADELINE C. GERWICK

Kevin owned a small retail store and decided to have a big promotion. It was a bit risky, but he wanted to attract new customers. He brought in extra inventory, paid for more advertising, and spruced up the store. He did everything right, yet something went wrong. On the day of the big sale, *no one came!* Not a single customer. Was it just bad luck, or perhaps a bad economy? That's usually how we frame such events. In this case, the "culprit" was *bad timing!*

Unfortunately, the date Kevin chose for his big sale was an all-day, Time-Out. These are times when nothing positive comes of a new start. There's no energy to push forward, or even to purchase things during these times.

In another situation, one day a major computer operations company had a *gigantic mess up* in their computers. It was such chaos that the primary technicians didn't even have a clue where to start. If they tried to unravel it, they might make the situation worse.

However, they had one thing which saved them. They both had a particular book which indicated they were in a Time-Out period and they were missing critical information. To their credit, they decided to *do nothing* until the Time-Out was over. It was going to clear within a few hours and since they had no idea what to do, this was their best option. Imagine their huge surprise when the Time-Out ended and the computer systems fixed themselves with no effort on their part!

These true stories give you a good sense of how important it is to utilize timing. It can make or break a company, no matter what size it is. Good timing was the secret advantage that JP Morgan used to become a billionaire. Walt Disney also used it to open his theme parks, sign contracts and introduce movies. Yet this advantage is one of the best-kept secrets in business.

Why does timing matter? Days are *not* created equal! Each day has different *qualities.* Some days are great for success and others are designed so that nothing will come of your actions (Time-Outs). Yes, it's true. The date/time you choose to take important actions impacts your success.

It's hard to imagine, isn't it? Yet, you wouldn't go to the beach at night to get a sun tan, or plant your garden in the middle of a cold winter. That's because you can easily observe sun cycles. However, there are many other cycles which also impact your success, and unfortunately, they're *not* visible.

Basically the Universe has a plan for how it wants us to use each day. This means that not all days are good days for doing important activities, for a promotion, giving a workshop, taking a trip, or doing a major mailing. Not all days are good for making sales calls, signing a contract, or launching a web site.

This may surprise you, because our culture thinks all days are equal. In fact, we're berated for "wasting" time when we're not productive. However, that's not how the Universe works and from its perspective, it's neither possible, *nor desirable,* to constantly be pushing forward. In nature, there are *no examples of constant activity without rest and renewal.*

What is timing? It's the study of universal cycles and energies, also known as astrology. During the Great Depression, President Roosevelt hired Edward Dewey to find out what cycles were causing it. Dewey discovered that *all* cycles were related to the movement of the planets in the heavens. He correctly identified the cycles related to the Great Depression and similar ones repeated during the 2008 financial crisis. He began the Foundation for the Study of Cycles based on his discovery.

Planets don't actually *cause* things to occur. Much like a thermometer, they *indicate* which energies are occurring, but they don't *cause* those energies. Everyone has free choice. Carl Jung, a psychologist and an astrologer, introduced the concept of the Universe being synchronous. He suggested that the energies occurring overhead with the planets are the same energies we simultaneously experience here on Earth. We can choose to ignore these energies, but they still impact us.

Now before we go any further, let's clear up some misinterpretations about astrology. In biblical times astrology was considered to show the Divine Plan of the Day. This was considered to be *much* more important than anyone's personal cycles. Even the Bible mentioned not to go to astrologers, fortune tellers or tea leaf readers. Why? It was considered crazy to think about your own personal cycles, instead of working in harmony with the Divine Plan of the Day.

It might surprise you to know that the largest astrological library in the world is at the Vatican. Even the Pope's throne is carved with astrological symbols. The Bible also talks about a time for every purpose under heaven, which was shown by astrology.

Certain parts of the world never forgot the Divine Plan of the Day. Asian cultures continued to use it to their great benefit. However, western society disregarded the Divine Plan of the Day about 400 years ago, when science got started. This is part of the ancient wisdom that our ancestors knew. We need this information now, more than ever, so we can understand what's really happening in our world. Important changes are occurring, and working with them is vital to our success.

MAJOR ECONOMIC CYCLES

With this basic understanding, let's discuss some major, economic cycles and two common cycles that impact your success on a regular basis. First, we're in the midst of very important, economic cycles occurring between 2000 and 2040. These rare cycles are associated with monumental changes.

In 2000, we began a 20-year cycle of economic and social revolution. (Jupiter conjunct Saturn in Taurus square Uranus in Aquarius). This would be a *lot* by itself. The last time it occurred was when the American

Civil War began. Over 600,000 men were killed and many more were disabled. The labor force was decimated and it took twenty years to redevelop it.

This same cycle recurs again in 2020, creating a total of forty years of economic revolution through 2040. The last time this cycle repeated itself was between 1047 and 1087, over 950 years ago. When you find rare cycles occurring, something big is up. This forty-year, economic revolution is the container for the rest of the major cycles that occur with it. This is the longest one, the overarching message.

What's important to understand about this economic revolution is that we're creating an *entirely new type of economy* during this forty-year period. Since 1841 we've had an economy based on agriculture, manufacturing, services, and financial products. That economy is changing to one based on information, data, communications, transportation, relationships, partnerships, alliances, innovation and technology. This new economy will last from 2020 until 2160. If you want to be successful, you need to align yourself with these changes.

PERMANENT ECONOMIC CHANGES

As part of the economic revolution, when the financial crisis began in 2008, we entered a 16-year period of economic transformation or permanent change (Pluto in the sign of Capricorn). This cycle occurs approximately once every 248 years. It last occurred between January 1762 and January 1778, when the US became a nation. This cycle ends November 19, 2024.

What's the purpose of these permanent, economic changes? To build a sustainable and healthy economy that will nurture ourselves and the Earth. At the moment, we don't have a sustainable economy, so a lot of structures must be changed. This process is similar to remodeling a house, tearing down walls, putting in new wiring and plumbing. Things are chaotic at first. However, they get much better over time.

Between 2010 and early 2019, we're also in a revolutionary period, when individuals take back their power and demand their rights (Uranus in Aries square to Pluto in Capricorn). Revolutionary energies are exploding globally. Leaders have been ousted; others have resigned. Anger is rampant. There have been protests worldwide, and many truths have been revealed. Revolutionary discoveries are occurring. Technologies and tools that have been suppressed for decades are being released. Things are changing! The way we do business is changing too.

TIME-OUTS

Let's now consider the impact of two common cycles on your success and prosperity. Have you ever taken an important action that didn't work out? If so, it wasn't due to bad luck. It was due to bad *timing!* Observing one cycle, called Time-Outs, will greatly increase your success and prosperity. This cycle occurs three times per week and lasts between a few minutes to over two days. On average it lasts five to ten hours.

In our culture, we believe we should go full speed ahead every day. However, the Universe has a different idea. It provides us time to rest, gestate our ideas, and finish things. It gives us cosmic, Time-Out periods for that purpose.

The meaning of these Time-Out periods is that *nothing comes of it.* When you attempt to start something new, make a decision, buy something, place an ad, do a mailing, close an important sale, or sign a contract during one of these periods, *nothing comes of it.* Just like in sports, you can't score, because the ball isn't in play. However, usually you don't realize this until *after* you've wasted a lot of time and money going down an erroneous path. Eventually you scrap it and have to start over.

About 25 years ago, the *Wall Street Journal* had an article about research done on bankrupt businesses. A group of astrologers randomly selected 1400 bankrupt companies and looked at their incorporation charts. They wanted to know if there was a common cycle that occurred in the charts of bankrupt companies. *They discovered that 100% of these businesses were incorporated during Time-Out periods* (void of course Moons) *and all of them went bankrupt.*

Imagine what happens when you unwittingly start a company, place an ad, hire someone, send out a mailing, purchase an important item, launch a web site, introduce a new product, or sign a contract during one of these Time-Out periods. Unfortunately, *nothing positive happens!*

If you make an important decision during these periods, you'll make the wrong one. During Time-Outs, you're either *missing or misunderstanding* some critical information. If you had that information or understood it correctly, you would make a different decision. You can avoid making failed decisions by waiting for a better time.

I once worked in a major electronics, test-equipment company, which seemed to have terrible timing. Yet they were the world-wide leader in their products. Whenever the company approved new product development programs during these Time-Out periods, the programs were *always scrapped*. After spending $250,000 to $500,000 on them, they would finally decide it wasn't going to work and cancel the program. Save your resources and get better results! Use good timing for important decisions.

How can you know when Time-Outs occur? You must have an astrological calendar. Otherwise these cycles appear random. The color-coded, *Good Timing Guide* is easy to use, and there are other astrological calendars available too.

MERCURY RETROGRADE

Another major cycle that impacts business is known as Mercury retrograde. Mercury represents our communications, documents and transactions, cars, transportation, schedules, computers, phones, emails, faxes, printers and other electronic equipment. During Mercury retrograde, the planet appears to slow down, stop, and move backwards for 3 to 3.5 weeks. Then it stops and slowly moves forward again. Since the cycles in the heavens reflect our energies on Earth, we experience delays and miscommunications.

Other pitfalls of Mercury retrograde are computers, tablets, phones and electronic equipment failures, travel problems, cars breaking down, delays in schedules, and printing problems. You're reconsidering your needs during this period. If you sign a contract, you may regret it later when you realize your needs are different. It's also common to find mistakes in contracts or misunderstand them.

Now why in the world would the Universe give us a cycle like this? These periods are designed to slow us down, to enable us to *catch up*, find and fix our mistakes, *and learn* something. However, in our culture, there's an odd expectation that if you're competent, you should never make a mistake! This is completely unrealistic. It wouldn't be very interesting either, because we wouldn't be learning.

Mercury retrogrades are the perfect time to fix things, reprint anything, redo or rework anything, re-plan and rewrite. They're also great times for catching up, doing research, looking back at the past, or re-connecting with family, friends or customers.

In order to be in harmony with this cycle, plan about 50% of what you normally schedule. This allows you time to catch up. When crises arise (mistakes that have to be fixed immediately), you can fit them into the open parts of your schedule. This prevents schedule changes as the crises appear, and makes it much less stressful.

This is not the time to start new projects or introduce new products, as everyone is in crisis mode and they're ignoring your direct mailings, emails, and product introductions. When a product or service is introduced during these periods, sales are normally 40% below forecasted sales. The only time I saw it work for a product introduction was when the movie, *Titanic* came out. This film looked back in history, so it was appropriate for the period and highly successful.

By the way, the Titanic set sail under Mercury retrograde and they forgot to bring any binoculars on board. In addition to being a Mercury item, binoculars would have allowed them spot the iceberg in time. This is an example of a Mercury retrograde mistake that literally *sank the ship*. Talk about a bad product introduction!

What should you do during these periods? Plan to catch up. It's very hard to do that if you're trying to start something new. Don't start new projects during these periods unless you're actually fixing or repairing something, cleaning or recycling items. It's a good time to re-connect with family and friends. For businesses, it's great to re-contact customers and remind them of existing products or services.

TIME FOR A REVOLUTION IN BUSINESS?

Revolutionary energies are underway! Isn't it time we had a revolution in business too? These are just a few of the ways timing can help us improve our success and businesses. Let's start working in harmony with the universal energies, rather than being in fear of what *might* happen. Once you understand how to co-create your world with the energies of the Universe, you'll stop wasting valuable resources with bad timing. Together we'll create enough abundance on this planet for everyone to be prosperous.

About Madeline

Madeline C. Gerwick is an internationally-recognized, business, economic, and personal astrologer, speaker and author. She has a BA degree with honors in Economics, and she's listed in several Who's Who books, including *Who's Who in the World*. She annually writes *The Good Timing Guide: Time Codes for Success*. She also joined well-known authors Steven Covey, Tom Peters, Oprah, Steve Jobs, Donald Trump, Thomas Moore, Scott Peck, Robert Kiyosaki and many more as contributing authors in the business anthology, *Einstein's Business, Engaging Soul, Imagination and Excellence in the Workplace*.

She's also taught prosperity training to business people since 2002. Co-facilitated with Margaret Donahue, their *8 Keys to the Ultimately Prosperous Business* trains companies to understand that money is a form of energy. As such, energy is the true bottom line of any business and all management is a form of energy management. Once companies understand how to better utilize their energy and work in harmony with the Universe, they can prosper in any economy.

Madeline co-authored *The Complete Idiot's Guide to Astrology*, available from Penguin Group and she's a featured, monthly guest on the Jeff Rense Show (www.renseradio. com). Her unique combination of credentials makes her an in-demand speaker regarding economic conditions, prosperity and good timing.

While working in business, she observed the synchronicity of astrological cycles associated with sales, project development, marketing, manufacturing, purchasing, legal issues, travel, contracts and more. Her combined experience in both astrology and business led to the development of her *Good Timing Guide*, to provide better productivity for all types of businesses.

Madeline provides businesses of all sizes excellent timing to help them hit home runs with new product introductions, launch web sites, sign important contracts or start new companies. Using a company's incorporation or LLC start date, Madeline provides cycles information for companies, including growth opportunities, financial outlooks, operations, legal, and marketing information, plus consolidation periods. This creates an accurate road map for the company's future and makes planning more effective. She also provides consultations to individuals.

Her company, Polaris Business Guides, is a consulting and training firm which guides organizations and individuals to prosper by working in harmony with the Universe.

Please visit her at: www.polarisbusinessguides.com

Or call her in Arlington WA, toll free at: 877-524-8300
Or internationally at: 360-474-1149.

You'll also find her on Facebook:
https://www.facebook.com/polarisbusinessguides

CHAPTER 18

FROM FED UP TO LIFTED UP
– MOVING PAST THE TORMENT AND FINDING FULFILLMENT

BY AMILIA POWERS

Nothing can hold us back more so than the fear of letting go.

To the outside world, I was "typical." A young woman, divorced, a mother to two small children—nothing really out of the ordinary. Getting married so young had led to getting divorced young. My husband and I both wanted to live different lives. It was an inevitable ending to something that had happened far too early in my life.

As I moved on with my life, I struggled financially, but I was determined to make it. I knew what I wanted. I stayed focused, saved and purchased a home—only to realize that it took a lot of money to maintain that home. I had to get a second job to better support myself and provide for the kids. There were no other options and I wanted everything to work out. Yet, nothing was great. Working wasn't my problem. I wasn't scared of hard work. It was when I started to date again that I found a big problem—I was more successful at attracting the wrong kind of men than I'd realized.

Time moved on and I met a man. He was wonderful and treated me the way every girl dreams of being treated. I mistook that for amazing love and unfortunately it turned into pain and torment. My fear of letting go consumed me, because I loved him and wanted it to work, all I felt and tried to hold onto was the day we met. I also had to settle for a second job that I didn't like, long dreadful hours that were physically exhausting, but felt I needed. I wasn't happy. I was trying to keep up appearances. There was no balance or harmony in my life—anywhere. Furthermore, knowing that I was responsible was agonizing. My life deteriorated and I struggled to stay under control. The more I fought, the more my life unraveled. I didn't like the person I turned into, becoming more distant from my life and never finding peace. I was just existing. It was time to get radical.

SHAKING IT UP AND REMOVING THE CLUTTER

When the voices inside your head are screaming that you need to make a change, listen.

"When did you have enough?" This is a question that has been asked to me by hundreds of people, whether face to face or via my blog. The answer: I needed to listen to my lesson that I was served. Let me explain what that means:

> I had been journaling for years, writing down day-to-day encounters, both good and bad, and how they impacted me. Everything was my journal, including the stories of friends, coworkers, and random individuals who had confided in me for some reason, sharing their lives' unfortunate experiences. Over the years and upon reflection on these entries, I saw a trend. There were similarities in everyone's story. Well, I'd wanted change for them and their happiness? So, what about me?

For me, journaling had begun as a way to help emotionally manage all the acts of verbal torment and unkindness that I had in my home life. It was a reprieve, and by unloading my feelings, my energy was restored just enough to tackle one more day. Well, our lives are made up of an awful lot of "one more days." I suddenly had to admit that if I was going to become more vested in a life than just a day I would need to take control for what was best for me.

Here was my reality:

- I had to work two jobs to keep money flowing into the household.
- The amount of stress that I was under was stifling.

- My health had suffered, my weight skyrocketing.
- I was the one allowing these things to happen.

Everything in my life was habit, but none of the habits were good. My mind was stuck, but my intuition was begging me to move on to where I should be. And I wanted to, but it took some conditioning. I knew what was happening. I had to:

- Focus my thoughts
- Address my fears
- Not back away from the changes I knew I needed

All the things that had led me to that low moment had been my fault. I enabled people in my life by giving them control over me. I had to be truthful to myself. This had to end, I wanted to breathe again. My resolve to stop the fighting, sleepless nights, and constant tears became stronger than my fear of standing up for myself. I had resolve!

ONE STEP AT A TIME

New air is breathed into us when we are freed from our self-inflicted negative situations.

When the relationship finally ended, no words can adequately describe the liberation I felt. I was instantly better and freed, no longer thinking about what had been. All the hard work that was ahead would not hold me back; it inspired me to move forward. All the answers didn't exist in me and to manage that, I prayed day-in and day-out for solutions and guidance, hoping my eyes, ears, and heart would be open to the life moments that would bring what I needed to me.

Through fear we can identify what we do not want in our lives.

Next, I quit my second job. It had been a source of misery with its long days and hours and I'd dealt with it long enough. No more! If I was going to need more income to support my family, it would have to come from a source that brought me satisfaction. However, these things would not have happened if fear had reigned supreme inside of me. When we eliminate fear, we:

- Allow our happiness to satisfy us more than we try to appease everyone else (which is impossible, as we cannot control others responses, only our own)
- Look forward to building a life, not just surviving a day
- Embrace the circumstances that used to hold us back, because we see the lessons in them
- Find resolutions more quickly and they feel right, even without convincing ourselves
- Eliminate the fear of mental torture and unkindness
- Create boundaries that don't allow people who are cruel to us into our personal space – we may have to deal with them, but they don't hold the power
- Are able to work on unconditional love for ourselves and grant ourselves the forgiveness that we need to move on

By doing all these things, we are using fear to our advantage. The tables turn and the results change. The cycle of insanity comes to an end.

With all the things I was going through, I almost felt like an infant who was learning to do everything for the first time—eyes wide open and curious. I slowly stopped doubting that I had the ability to overcome any obstacle that came my way. There was this instinctual awareness that understood the bad behaviors and patterns that could lead to falling back into "the old patterns." I took my identity back by:

- Enjoying and embracing the process of rediscovering me
- Making conscious choices to appreciate who I was and what I did offer this world
- Aligning my life with my goal, which was to bring value to the world
- Refusing to be taken advantage of

All of the things I did are exciting to say and they sound well, but they can be tough to achieve. I admit that. You need to break down old habits and create new ones that help guide you toward what you wish to achieve. I found that a large part of what was required to do all of these things came from acknowledging that I did have intuition and it was there for a reason.

USING INTUITION AS OUR GUIDE

We are all born with intuition. It is a guiding force that is a part of us and can lead to better choices.

Most of us can reflect on a time when we thought, *I knew that I shouldn't have done that. Now look what's happened.* Our intuition was strong and bold, letting us know that what we were about to do wasn't a good idea. We didn't listen. We wanted it and took what we thought would help the "present moment" with no regards to it being a temporary fix or something that would have a detrimental effect down the road. Only to regret it. So much negative energy, time, and worry could have been removed if we'd just embraced our intuition.

The beautiful thing about intuition is that our own intuition is not selfish or deceitful, it is just there to serve our best interests. Yet we abandon it, strong arming it with our freewill and sometimes that search for instant gratification. When ignored, intuition goes into hiding. But it's also forgiving and will come back out quickly to help us!

By freeing our intuition we gain clarity and strength. The risks of falling into old patterns and habits that were detrimental to our hearts, as well as our minds, will lessen. Boundaries are in place and our intuition reinforces it.

- Hateful people stop plaguing our mind and draining our thoughts.
- The power others have over our pasts doesn't carry into the present and future—we are freed from the chains of their control.
- We tap into our endless power source to help us change and transform our life.

There are only lessons to be learned. We are the creators of our experience, so when we start adjusting our thinking to acknowledge this truth we begin to transform our own lives. Through writing our own narrative, we are driven by love, kindness, respect, joy, and peace. We have gratitude and thanks for all the things that are forming our life. Those times when all we hoped for was "just surviving the day" become rarer, a distant memory that still carries an impactful lesson.

COMING FULL CIRCLE

Shedding the "victim mentality" liberates the mind and brings about wonderful transformations.

Taking a deliberate effort to refuse to take on the victim mentality or allow other to give you the title is tough, but necessary. For me, I balanced that line many times over many years, but I stood strong against it. If I could do it, why couldn't others? It was that thought that led me to where I am today. Knowing that my experiences and rebound to a better place—a wonderful, fulfilled, passion-driven life was something that I knew was meant to be shared—my payback to the world around me and all those people who were truly hurting.

Today, as an Inspirational Coach, I help both men and women look at their situations and begin to make the changes that will free them from mentally, physically, and/or emotionally- tortured lives that are overflowing with unkindness. And people have responded to it, wanting more and reaching out to me. Every one of them is important to me and whether we are one-on-one or connected through the community I've created at: www.ValueUrSelf.com, I help people reconnect with their intuition and establish the barriers and recognition of what their life can be—but they're behind the wheel. I can guide them, but only they can get themselves there.

My approach is different and to give you an idea of how it might play out, I wanted to share an example with you. Someone came to me very recently, a man—yes, men are the victims of horrible experiences at the hands of spouses, too—and he was a kind guy, had a great job, worked hard, and loved his wife completely. His entire identity was wrapped around her and the thought of leaving his wife made him think that he'd be severing himself from love itself. The fear of loss was overwhelming. To help him gain some perspective I asked some questions, such as:

- What is the cost of making this CHOICE?
- Are you happy living in FEAR?
- Is this the way you want to SHARE your love?
- Is this the LIFE you really want?

I wanted him to be true to himself. He answered these questions honestly. I was able to show him that love cannot die and love is not a person, it lives in all of us. It's an emotion that can never be taken away. We need to understand our value and have control of our lives and what we allow in it to have a more meaningful, loving experience. He loved his wife, but truthfully, he'd gone through enough. She no longer made him light up with joy and happiness. He lived in defense mode, assuming he'd have to counter whatever cruel intention she had in mind—always. How exhausting!

This man's story is like many peoples' stories. We attach our value and love to the wrong things. To change it means we take a step forward each and every day. Some of these steps may be easy and others may be hard—but we keep going and trying and before we know it, our intuition is helping us, our current situations have a better perspective, loving ourselves changes everything.

Our lives are our reality—not the rosy one we may pretend exists, but what really happens day to day and how it makes us feel. That's where the quality of how we live is defined. Helping guide people to the life that gives them sparks, hopes, love, and emotional freedom is what I do. And I would have never guessed how many people crave this in their lives. The outpouring of stories and pleas for help is touching, which is all a part of my purpose as a human and as an Inspirational Coach.

HEALING AND LIVING IS A GLOBAL ISSUE
No matter where someone lives, the human condition of NOT "loving thyself" will always exist.

Through the years I've been just as honored as I was compelled to help individuals heal from the hurt that they are carrying inside of them. I'm in this wonderful place where everything has come together and I have access to people that need help. Being there for them means everything to me. That is why finding a way to strengthen my outreach by creating this online community, as well as group efforts, to help people come together is already working—and helping others! There is so much hurt in this world and helping people learn the lessons they can from that means they are healing. A healthier emotional world will become a safer world for many of the smallest communities in the world—the family home.

About Amilia

With a passion-driven focus to help others, Amilia Powers is a very active person who is highly committed in her role as an Inspirational Coach. Through her work, she works with clients in either individual or group settings and forums to help them in their life's transitions. Amilia sees that there are no regrets necessary in life, only opportunities to learn from mistakes that are the result of wrong choices. With this at the heart of her inspirational healing and transformational practices, her commitment to finding a way to reach out to anyone in need as they navigate through the challenges of their life and find the courage to begin new life chapters that are grounded in boundaries, self-awareness, and self-love, she has begun a global movement.

Today, a universal audience visits Amilia's interactive blog world, **(www.AmiliaPowers. blogspot.com)**. Through this site, she connects with people to help show them the standards that are required to live a more meaningful life. In Amilia's words, "I like to teach individuals the importance of self-value; the understanding of how this can help us make better choices to create more loving and happier experiences."

Over the years, Amilia has had many mentors who have taught her valuable lessons and strategies about how to make a true impact on other people. Brian Tracy is one such man, and through his motivational speeches he has offered great insight on how to help people move past all obstacles and find success. Tony Robbins has also offered great inspiration with his attitude of just "do it." Every day is a chance for a new lesson and an opportunity to extend her life experiences and commitment to Inspirational Coaching to someone in need. Amilia always remembers words that Oprah Winfrey, referencing having passion in your heart allows you to use it as a special gift to reach out to others. This aligns perfectly with Amilia's visions and life goals.

Amilia has also been quite active in Toastmasters International, a wonderful non-profit platform that has given her the skills necessary to effectively speak in public and develop the confidence in sharing her mission with others. Now she is also excited to add Best Selling Author to this list, having created a chapter in *Success Manifesto*, which is co-authored with her mentor, Brian Tracy. Her inspirational book, *Pain Behind Broken Vases*, has a release date of July 2016 and will be followed up with *The New Chapter* in October 2016. Amilia was recently interviewed for the TV show *Times Square Today* as well. Times Square Today will be appearing on CNN, CNBC, and Fox News affiliates around the country in Fall 2016.

Amilia is passionate about the power of family and cherishes the opportunities to connect with her parents, son and daughter, and her five grandchildren, which are a constant source of laughter and joy for her. And to all who ask her what her best nugget of wisdom is, she often says, "When we understand how important it is to value one's self, it change the dynamics of our lives."

You may connect with Amilia at:
- www.AmiliaPowers.blogspot.com
- www.ValueUrSelf.com
- Facebook, Twitter, and Google+: ValueUrSelf
- LinkedIn
- AmiliaPowers@gmail.com.

CHAPTER 19

YOUR FOCUS WILL DETERMINE YOUR OUTCOME

BY ANGELENA LEWIS

An important key to success is having strategies that can help you to stay focused and persevere when setbacks inevitably occur.

When it comes to achieving our goals, people often tell you to go for it and don't stop until you make it. The trouble with this well-meaning advice is that the people giving it rarely understand the trials you are likely to face in pursuit of that goal.

Yes, between where you are right now and where you want be is a whole lot of what I like to call setbacks. These setbacks aren't there to discourage us but to help us to grow into the person we need to be in order to succeed. However, they can sometimes be so emotionally distressing that they stop us in our tracks.

In this chapter, I am going to share with you my own journey to success and some strategies that I hope will give you the tools you will need to overcome the setbacks, and achieve success in any endeavour you might choose.

Now success means different things to different people so I think it is important to define what is meant when I speak of success. When I speak of success, I'm not referring to attainment of wealth, fame or status commonly understood as success (though this may indeed come with it), instead, I speak of the outer manifestation of an inner desire or intention.

As a result, the story I share with you today is not your typical success story, but a very personal weight loss journey which reflects within it a vital component to success.

Four months ago, I set myself the goal of losing two stone (28 pounds) in three months. I had decided that I was going to lose weight by engaging in healthier eating, exercising more and I wanted to make these changes a habit. This desire came from a deep need to feel good, have more energy, experience more vitality. If I am completely honest this desire had been playing on my mind for months, but only when the pain of staying the same became too great was I prepared to take actions necessary to make a change.

Looking back on it now, the only reason I hadn't taken action earlier was because I was too busy telling myself 'a bunch of reasons' why I could not do it. These 'reasons' aka excuses, whilst they helped me to feel better about my lack of action in the short term actually kept me in a state of helplessness that would only ensure further weight gain. However, it wasn't my weight gain that lead me to finally take action (in fact I personally didn't think there was anything wrong with the way I looked). It was my lack of energy, the constant nagging of my mind to take action and general lack of vitality for life that made me finally decide enough was enough.

My plan started out well. I replaced my daily desktop chocolate feasts with nuts or sunflower seeds, cut out all obviously fattening foods such as chips and burgers, replaced them with healthier alternatives and attended gym classes three to four times per week. Even though I had opted to weigh myself only once per month, I could already feel the benefits of my efforts in just a few weeks.

Yes, it was all going well until I was challenged by the Xmas holidays; over this two-week period, I stopped attending classes and proceeded to eat and drink alcohol without restriction – this is what people do at Xmas wasn't it? The result was, at the end of the first month, I had only lost a pound in weight.

When it is obvious that a goal cannot be reached, don't adjust the goals, adjust the action steps.
~ Confucius

Now, with only two months to achieve the same goal, it was clear that if I had any chance of achieving it, I would have to employ a more intense approach. I no longer had the time for trial and error, but needed a tried-and-tested formula. So I took a leaf out of my own 'goal-achieving' handbook and consulted Edel Keenehan, (known on social media as Bikini buff) a certified personal/online trainer, and a successful NPC and IFBB bikini athlete.

Edel was great, she took into account my goal then gave me an eating regime and adjusted my exercise regime to suit, replacing my gym classes with a weight training and cardio workout that was more robust yet still within my capabilities. My new eating regime consisted of a healthy balanced diet of both proteins and good carbohydrates and also required that I prep my meals ahead of time. This freed up an incredible amount of time and energy for other things and also reduced my exposure to temptation. One of the reasons for my first setback was that I found it so hard to resist the temptation of unhealthy foods, but having meals that were always available when I needed them now made it much easier to stick to the plan and "say no" to other less healthy options.

Another reason for this setback (apart from the obvious splurge), was because I hadn't received enough feedback about my progress, or lack of, throughout. So now, along with sending weekly reports of my progress to Edel, I weighed myself every morning. This served as a benefit for many reasons, it brought my goal to the forefront of my conscious mind every morning and helped me to focus on the positive steps I needed to take that day. It gave me feedback on the action I had taken the previous day and it also equipped me with motivation to keep going.

In just a couple of weeks, my new eating, exercise and morning regime had induced what I like to call 'the flow', in which I was now eating the right things and exercising with consistency and focusing on my goal without much conscious effort. As a result, I was losing weight with ease, looking good, feeling great and getting a step closer to reaching my goal every day.

Yes, I was officially on a roll until a birthday celebration at an all-you-can-eat buffet. My initial response to this invitation was a resolve to take a set meal with me, but later decided against it. Bringing my own meal wouldn't look right and besides, I'd replaced a meal for other healthy options in the past during a social event or two with no adverse effects, so I figured I could handle it, I was wrong.

The next day, after consuming what I considered to be a sensible amount of protein, carbs and a very thin slice of cake, I found that I'd gained three extra pound and I was gutted!! Yes, I believe this is the best word I could use to describe the emotion, because I had such a hollow feeling in my stomach that it literally felt as though my intestinal organs had been removed.

With just over six weeks left, and a three-pound weight gain that pushed me back up to 12.02, after breaking the 12-stone barrier, this felt like a huge setback, and if I am completely honest, my mind could only think of two options, go on a starvation diet to get rid of the extra pounds as quickly as possible or go eat three pizzas and just forget about the whole thing. Whilst the starvation approach presented the illusion of being more optimistic than the second, it was in fact no more so, as it would mean quitting on the idea of losing the weight in a healthy way and this aspect of the goal was so important to me that to compromise on it would make the success completely invalid.

Once I understood that none of those options would bring me much success, I decided to do the only thing that was left, take responsibility. I knew that taking responsibility for all my actions (not just the ones that yielded favourable results), was the only path that would lead to success. So within a couple of hours, I managed to accept the situation for what it was and the part I played. It interrupted the 'you've-got-no-chance-now', 'whatever-you-try-is-useless', 'you- are-helpless' tape I was allowing to run in my mind, by forcing me to ask myself what my next positive action should be. I then focused on that next action.

As a result, I immediately put myself back onto my eating regime, this time with even more commitment and a 'no excuses, no swaps' attitude, continued my exercise regime and weighing myself every morning. But now, instead of allowing the regret of the three-pound weight gain and the echo of helplessness to seep into my mind, I got onto the scales and said out-loud, 'I have the power to effect positive change', 'My positive actions lead to positive outcomes', and 'I am in full control'. In less than a week, I was losing weight, looking great and back on the path directed towards success.

A week before my deadline, I was faced with yet another celebration dinner, this time at one of my favourite restaurants. Fortunately, having already learnt the lessons needed to succeed from the last setback, I overcame it with flying colours, sticking to my regime to the letter.

A week later, a total of three months after beginning my challenge, I weighed in at 10 stone, eight pounds and though my target weight was 10 stone 5 pounds, I was winner. I'd managed to drop a total of 1 stone 11 pounds (25 pounds) in eight weeks by eating a healthy diet and working out consistently five days per week. Clothes that used to just hang in my wardrobe as decoration now fit with ease. My confidence soared, though not so much from the weight loss but from the level of dedication and follow through I'd applied throughout the task. I had more energy, more flexibility, more agility and even better skin.

Today, as I write this, I smile even wider as I realize that not only did I change my eating habits and increase my activity, but these changes have indeed become something I continue to practice regularly . . . a way of life . . . a habit.

Though I did make a few errors in judgement regarding my eating habits, the hardest part of my challenge was, having to continually overcome what I consider the number one reason for failure, setbacks.

So next I'm going to share with you some strategies to help you stay focused when the going gets tough.

1) Identify the problem

Look your setback square in the eye and ask yourself, what was the cause? Be honest, was it a failure to commit or adapt? Whatever it was, identify it. A lot of people try to deny any setbacks, this is the worst thing we could do, because if it didn't happen we can't learn from it and if we can't learn from it, we can't grow into the kind of person we need to be in order to win.

2) Own it

Take responsibility for your part; no, this doesn't mean have yourself a grand pity party to replay all your *shoulda, coulda, woulda's* or making up a load of excuses for why you can't succeed. This is draining and doesn't yield positive results. Conserve your energy for the next round by acknowledging your power in the situation and identifying what you might have done to contribute to the setback, then decide how you will use that power to achieve more positive results in the future.

3) Stop the tape

When you encounter a setback, you can pretty much guarantee that you will have a tape playing in your mind about it – most of the time this tape is focused on what we don't want rather than what we do, and we are not even aware that it is playing. Yet it is this very tape that kills many of our dreams before they have any chance of becoming a reality. It was Wayne Dyer who once said:

No one has ever died from a snake-bite. They die from the venom which continues to pour through the system long after the bite took place.

This tape is like the venom that continues to flow through our system long after the setback has occurred, and is the reason for much failure in life.

The trick is to use affirmations to interrupt this tape, enough to enable us to do Step 4), and then, once we begin to experience positive results from that action, to use affirmations to reinforce a new, more positive tape that will fuel motivation and further success.

4) Re-strategies

Take stock of your current situation, what you have learnt and any nagging feelings from within, and then decide from where you stand what your next positive action should be.

5) Re-execute - Take that positive action

6) Repeat steps 1 - 5 - with every setback you encounter until you succeed.

The steps that I have shared with you today will ensure that you have the tools to stay focused and keep on, keeping on even when the road gets rocky.

The key to success is to stay focused and take practical action, knowing that the real challenge is in continually overcoming setbacks and adjusting your course, until those inner desires and intentions become an outer reality.

So often, when we encounter setback, we tell ourselves that we have failed, yet it is this very illusion that threatens our success. We must not fall prey to this deception, but instead, understand that a failure to attempt is the only failure that truly exists, everything else is progress.

About Angelena

After achieving many of her own personal and professional goals, Angelena Lewis is now a Personal Development Coach, Author, Inspirational Speaker and the founder of LIVIN FOCUS.

Providing Focus Coaching, online training, workshops and inspirational speeches, she encourages individuals and groups to address the personal challenges in their lives, break down disempowering beliefs and begin the journey towards becoming their best selves.

Her mission is to ensure that individuals have access to the kind support and motivation that encourages mental, spiritual and emotional growth.

To find out more about Angelena and Livin Focus:

Visit: www.livinfocus.com,
Or call: +44 117 3534606
Or email: angelena@livinfocus.com

CHAPTER 20

VICTORY CODE
– RELENTLESS REBOUNDING AND THE SIX STEPS TO WINNING BIG

BY MICHAEL S. POLLACK

INTRODUCTION

Few things in my life have put me through such a rigorous and challenging learning experience as caring for my first child, starting a (fully legitimate and legal) business, and making poor choices, causing my family and me to become homeless. Out of those three, two were very positive, yet scary mountains to climb—starting a business and caring for a newborn baby were strenuous and tough, but I was inspired and that inspiration carried me quite a long way. The other was far more powerful—yet, very negative, and very bad feeling. Causing my family to become homeless and for me to feel like a complete loser had no inspiration in it at all, but the experience was certainly loaded with motivation out of that disgust and desperation. Nothing has ever been so bad, yet so good for me all at the same time because this led to an ascent in my life like I've never experienced—a self-education of sorts, and discovering *"The Six Steps to Winning Big"*:

1. **Eyes on the Prize:** Identify major outcomes that make you sizzle just thinking about them!

2. **Carving out Time:** Breaking the prize down into bite-sized pieces.

3. **Laser-like Focus:** Eradicating distractions and controlling your attention so you can set the perfect aim.

4. **Measuring Up:** Documenting your current situation in order to measure, change, and easily improve your future.

5. **Record/Review the Tapes:** Document your personal history – your ideas, problems, and solutions – on paper.

6. **All Out Beast Mode!:** Defined, it simply means, "Take Action!"

You are born with none of these above skills—they are all easily learned, practiced and honed skills that any able human can quickly apply. My goal is to open peoples' eyes and spread the realization that we really need to be learning and teaching about these other, less popular subjects that I never learned about in school in such a way. This Victory Code could very quickly revolutionize everything for anyone who learns and applies these simple fundamentals.

EYES ON THE PRIZE

INSIGHT: What is the easiest way to make it through a maze? Begin at the end instead of at the beginning. The pathway is shockingly easy to see when you begin from the end.

The simple definition is the same as the actions we need to take to achieve a goal:

(i). List things we want to accomplish,

and...

(ii). Set a deadline for its accomplishment.

That is merely what we do every time we plan our week/day as well—we are setting goals on a much smaller scale for that day or that week.

We cannot achieve something that we don't believe in because we cannot see its completion in our minds, and not because we cannot visualize what it looks like in the end, but because we cannot see an actual path to its completion. Usually, until we can see a *path* in our minds, then there is no path, and we will not reach the goal. The reason we work backward from a goal is to find a path from another direction because we can see roadblocks more clearly and ways around them.

As long as we see a path then we have a path, and we now can get to the finish line. It is almost 100% certain that you will not get to that finish line on the *first* path you envisioned. You just have to know and understand that as long as you see a way, then you are able to get there. You can super-empower your vision of the path by having a very strong reason "Why" you need to reach this goal.

Victory Tactics:
How to figure out what's important and who you really want to be:

1. If you died right now, what would your eulogy reveal to the world about you?

2. What do you really want it to say?

3. Write it down.

CARVING OUT TIME

INSIGHT: In order to be effective you have to have a target in place first so that you have something to aim for.

I've heard it said that "Time Management is the real secret of the rich." It's not really a secret, but the *value* of it sure seems to be. Once we understand that time *is* the only equalizer we all share—nobody gets more than 24 hours/day—it really is about what we choose to do with those hours that makes or breaks us. It is a simple conclusion from there to do the things that make us and avoid those that break us.

Capture everything that requires any follow-up action from you. If it needs to be filed, file it—don't pile it. If it needs follow-up, schedule the call/appointment/email, task, etc. If it needs attention or action in any way, put it on your schedule and complete it before it is due. You need to have a notepad/phone, etc. at all times so that you can properly capture and schedule everything.

Victory Tactics:
Weekly & Daily Planning
- Keep a Master List (capture anything requiring action from you);
- Break your *Top 3*, one-year goals down to quarterly, monthly, weekly, & daily priorities that move you toward the mark;
- Before you start your week, add the most *vital* items onto your weekly schedule from your Master List (priority tasks & appointments) and spread them throughout your week accordingly;
- Schedule the lesser important, yet necessary tasks into the left-over spaces;
- Rewrite your Master List;
- Use your planning sheets as your mandatory, daily guide;
- Daily: Update your schedule and list to make sure your days stay on track and you miss nothing; *take excellent care that your vital items are worked on and completed before any and all others!*

LASER-LIKE FOCUS

INSIGHT: The acronym, "Follow One Course Until Successful" and forcing its application into your days is as vital to the process as it is for you to deeply understand the "must" of this behavior in order to see the power it has.

There is an endless barrage of information coming at us far more than ever before and marketers are all competing for one thing—our attention. Understanding this should cause some pause and thought as to what that could possibly mean. If our attention is that important to them shouldn't we consider how much more valuable it could be for us to focus that attention on our own wants, desires, and outcomes? These people know and understand very, very well that where our attention goes, our energy—and money—flows. The thing we pay most attention to is what gets our time, loyalty, and dollar. It's time to stop focusing on other's wonders and start creating our own.

A Focus Burst is a system I created that produces the best results and covers the most ground toward my goals each day; commit to it. I've tried many of these. There was this "one-hour on, one-hour off" system and others say, "90 minutes a day" or "90 minutes twice daily" and the list goes on. Some were very difficult to schedule and others I couldn't make sense of; I've never understood as to how you got anything done for taking such large chunks of time off for these "one-on/one-off" deals.

In all of its simplicity, this system involves us committing to items on our list that are the most critical, vital items and focusing for forty-five minutes at a time on *only* that. All of our days are based on hours and our work schedules are gauged by the same, so it is simple to plan our days around our hours. You have to stick this out to see just how fast you will surpass people all around you!

Victory Tactics:
Focus Burst: 45 minutes on; 15 minutes on something else.
- Set a timer for 45 minutes then wage all-out warfare on what you have lined up.
- Shut your door, close your email, *silence* your phone (not vibrate, turn it *off* or use airplane mode if you wish to use your phone's timer).
- Once the timer goes off: Check your phone for voicemails, follow up on emails, set up your next Focus Burst for the top of the hour, and repeat each hour possible.

MEASURING UP

INSIGHT: Measuring Up allows you to most efficiently realize if your goals are on track or headed for the cliff.

I can only cover one area in this paragraph, so I'm choosing finances, but this works in everything. Everyone should have a spending budget; if you don't, you need to get online and find one that makes sense—they're free. Your goals should include finances and you should have a spending, saving, and investing budget as well as a plan to make sure you're on track with each. The easiest form of measuring finances is by logging into your bank and reviewing transactions. There you can see where you met and missed budget items, but everything can be measured—and what gets measured *always* improves.

Victory Tactics:
Measure everything you wish to change—some apps make it easier:
- Health: Measure nutrients, calories, exercise, weight ("My Fitness Pal" app).

- Wealth: Create budget, purchase on debit cards only if possible, but capture everything ("Personal Capital" app keeps accounts in one place).
- Family/Relationships: Measure your undivided face-to-face time with your spouse/kids, and the relationships you most wish to cultivate. Your discovery here may shock you most.
- Spiritual: Log your meditation/prayer/devotion and action times.
- Mental: Capture the time you spend learning—classes/seminars/audio programs/reading.

RECORD/REVIEW THE TAPES

INSIGHT: Parents gain ground and should start their children off where the parents left off, not back where they started. Recording your journey is a brilliant treasure to leave for your children to make sure they don't backslide.

Documenting your own personal history—capturing your problems, solutions, wins/losses, ideas, events, major happenings in your world, having something to go back to even years prior that may solve your new problems, something to bring you back through your journey to see how far you've come and grown, keeping your children at the forefront of the newly-gained ground—is all the essence of Recording and Reviewing the Tapes. Don't miss the great opportunity to leave your family with your well-documented story as so many of the past have done to leave clues for the rest of us.

What would we have done if people didn't record math problems they couldn't solve or didn't carve words into stones and on paper for the rest of the world to learn from? Don't miss your chance at setting up your and your family's futures.

Victory Tactics:
Record and Review:
- Daily: What happened, ideas, problems, solutions, who you met, how you felt;
- Weekly: Put the week together as a whole, summarize the positive and negative;
- Monthly/Quarterly: Put together as a whole, summarize the positive and negative;

- Yearly: Review your past journals, up to five years, so you keep the items fresh; summarize the positives and negatives.

ALL OUT BEAST MODE

INSIGHT: "Action" is the catalyst that, when injected into the other Five Steps, causes the explosion that blasts your dreams into a sky high reality for the world to see.

Nobody has ever boiled it down better than the old marketers at Nike: "Just Do It." Going All Out Beast Mode on my dreams is *finally* what delivered me from desperation. Taking action is what made all of my goals become real. Unless you really go Beast Mode with the intent of seeing just what it can do for you, then you will not believe the great outcomes that *will* begin to pile up, especially when practiced daily and even over just a short period of time. What's even better is that once the habit forms you no longer need to force the action.

Seeing your results actually becomes addicting. I remember when I first started really hitting the gym hard when I was around 19 years old, walking in there for the first time wanting to make major muscle upgrades. Once I started seeing the results for myself (and even more motivating was when others would comment and confirm my suspicions) *IT WAS AWESOME!* Not too many things feel as rewarding as when others notice the changes that you went out and created; it is also very inspiring. Consequently, nothing has been more demeaning than people noticing you made changes for the worse and they lose their faith, belief, hope, and trust in you. Discipline, and the lack thereof, is always evident and obvious to anyone and everyone that comes in contact with you. You cannot fake it because no matter how hard you try, you are not fooling anyone; you are mature and make adult decisions, or you don't and anyone can see that.

You can have the best written goals ever designed, the best plan of action the world has ever seen, the best time-management plan, an excellent and simple tracking system, the biggest and coolest looking and smelling leather-bound, *empty* journal out there; and you could have the best forms and worksheets—which I provide for free to the public—but without the life blood of action/discipline you have nothing, except maybe a bunch of empty forms and journal pages, and possibly bank accounts and relationships.

We have all had successes in one thing or another; no matter these successes, they can be traced back to the action which we applied to each success.

Victory Tactic:

- Don't waste a moment! Go All Out Beast Mode until you've won!

FINAL THOUGHTS

Victory Code is a roadmap on how to master anything and to do it in record time. This stuff really works—you just have to work it. You always have to do your part. Greatness never comes freely; success and winning never come freely. This is here for those who really want it and are willing to take action to see their dreams become reality.

Beware of complacency. I've learned that complacency actually isn't a "comfort zone" at all—it's *confinement*—a prison we put ourselves in. I heard a pastor say, "Complacency comes from inattention and carelessness" and I believe he's right. We have to be very attentive and deliberate in our days—we don't have that many of them.

It's not about what anyone else does—we have no control over what they do. It's about what I am and what you are going to do to change our current circumstance no matter where we may be right now. I leave myself no other choice or outcome than winning and you can easily make that same choice for yourself.

No matter the size of any goal achieved, our faith in this process grows proportionately each time and some of us will be just curious enough to blow the whole lid off this entire thing—this life experience—and to see what the human potential really can be. Many have done it before; are you next?

About Michael

Michael Pollack helps income property owners across Southern California reach their income and retirement goals by efficiently running their businesses, and by that same token, he provides housing for families and effectively coordinates their housing needs.

Although operations didn't run so proficiently in previous businesses and ventures, Michael still saw accomplishments in many of the objectives he worked toward. Because he had not fully realized the mechanisms necessary to measure these sporadic victories, nor did he quite understand the mechanics of how these accomplishments were achieved, he too did not fully realize how to sustain these successes. With the many ups and downs he was experiencing and still unable to crack the Victory Code, it was finally the guilt of the quickly fading promises to his family that led him on an unrelenting pursuit to ultimately discovering The Six Steps to Winning Big, and realizing the immense power and speed of positive change that implementing the Victory Code would have on his life. What soon followed was the birth of Michael's third baby—the award-winning WestStar Property Management, Inc.

Starting with an 86% occupancy level and a 15% delinquency factor when the doors of WestStar first opened, Michael, applying the proven system of the Victory Code, led the team to an overall portfolio-wide occupancy level of 98% along with a delinquency factor of 3% in the first six months of operation, while doubling the size of the portfolio in the first eight months, paving the way for a first year revenue stream of over one million dollars.

His extensive commitment to and obsession for success in all areas of life is only preceded by his drive and passion for the building of good, strong relationships with clients, team members, vendors, local and state government officials, residents, and even his competitors! Michael is the driving force behind the operations of WestStar, its policies, procedures, and training, as well as the Rock*Star staffing WestStar enjoys.

Mr. Pollack also devotes time working as a volunteer Director and Committee Member for the esteemed, non-profit Apartment Association, California Southern Cities. Here Michael is working with long time experts, lawmakers, property owners, local residents, and community leaders, helping to make Southern California a better place to live and own property by helping to educate and bring understanding to the different views and realities about rental housing throughout the area.

Michael has a strong focus on learning and sharpening his skills through consistent application of the Victory Code principles and sharing it with others. As a dedicated husband and father of two, he enjoys working with families and developing ways to combat poverty therefore strengthening the fabric of our society—family. He enjoys spending time giving classes, speaking at churches, events, and homeless shelters, providing vision, personal coaching, and guidance to groups and individuals alike.

Connect with Michael today:

WestStar: www.weststarproperty.com
                michael@weststarproperty.com

Victory Code: www.michaelscottpollack.com

CHAPTER 21

MAXIMIZING eBUSINESS POTENTIAL
– PAVING THE WAY FOR VIRTUAL LAYAWAY

BY CASSANDRA BACKUS

Most retail sectors are missing out on one of the largest sources of online business...and they don't even know it!

Today's retail sectors face a plethora of challenges; none greater than harnessing consumer demand to empower business growth and tap into the billions of online eBusiness dollars in the retail sector. *This is missed revenue!* Until now, there has never been an easy platform for businesses, ranging in size from single proprietorships to corporate conglomerates, to have equal opportunities to offer the service of layaway to their consumers.

Now a new kid is on the block—a vLay pages tool called Virtual Layaway (vLay).

Virtual Layaway works effectively and smartly because it embraces a layaway software technology that uses the virtual online transaction, delivering the same results as a physical layaway. There is no longer a need to "accept" that layaway income is not a part of your virtual e-tail world. Because it is! This is a game changer when it comes to competing with "big box stores." In summary, this is what happens when you use

Virtual Layaway:
You will upload your best eCommerce products onto vLay pages, which may be listed out on your Website, eCommerce store, Shopify, Amazon, etc. You simply upload a link that takes you to layaway services and from there, the opportunities for more business take flight.

This technology is going to open up new opportunities for e-tail businesses to find greater success. You have the products people want and now they can purchase them on terms more favorable to them with Virtual Layaway, and the results are creating a shift in the paradigm of how online business can be conducted. This is exciting! What's next?

Understanding and engaging consumer purchasing preferences is key.

Layaway has been a key sales preference for many retailing years. However, technology has dwarfed physical layaway, making it a senseless waste of hard earned retail dollars. In the retail setting, the process of layaway takes away cash flow for up to six months, while the product is being purchased. This is ludicrous, and certainly not necessary. With Virtual Layaway, the same results are delivered while keeping cash flow available and working. This is the sales component of this option of the future. What about the consumer component?

There is an evolution of the consumer right in our face(book). For businesses, it's challenging for many of them to understand customers and their preferences in light of this rapidly changing virtual world. Because consumers have changed "foot-wise."

Businesses must adjust and flow with the demand for online purchasing.

We all know why! Factor in the things we love, such as convenience, with the horrid holiday and daily rush traffic, and a virtual solution will trump a drive to the store almost every time! So don't look down at your feet. They may look more webbed than in the past. Are you a web-footed online shopper? How about your customers?

There is an increasing consumer-driven demand to be able to make more purchases online.

Yes, we all have web feet and that population is growing. Just Google "foot traffic decline" and you can see over 986,000 results about this exact topic. Malls, large retail stores, and all the smaller chains and independently own stores are meeting struggles as their brick and mortar buildings complete with the web. It's a harsh reality—if you, the retail business, cannot harness your segment of the online business, you will not be in business, futuristically speaking.

To stay in business, you must offer the consumer every advantage within the shopping experience and online sale. The process must be co-mingled with the latest sales tools and social engagements, because that's where your customers are! This is possible with the use of tools such as Virtual Layaway. It adds value to the online shoppers purchasing experience. And layaway has proven to sustain businesses for decades but the face of shopping has changed with the Internet's rise. Therefore, layaway must change, as well.

The next retail paradigm is happening right now, before our very eyes. Are you paying attention to the evolution of retail to e-tail?

New businesses can no longer set up a brick and mortar location without connectivity to the "cyber world" and expect success. It will not happen, which means that every business plan has to include strategies for eBusiness. If not, business growth is not sustainable.

The term "e-tail" is electronic retailing, and it is growing at a rapid pace! With e-tailing, technology is used to empower customer service, as well as customer engagement. As a retailer, you must constantly reevaluate the digital landscape of your business footprint to stay abreast of the most up-to-date customer engagement software to have the tools necessary to ensure the best purchasing experience. This is the cutting-edge trend, but more than that, it's also the way of the future. There will be no going back.

To implement optimal digital interaction with your consumers, deliver what the customer wants in the most convenient way, and allow them the best digital experience while making a purchase.

The key strategic model that will grow your business involves implementation beyond the basic offline store with an online website.

You must implement a Real Time Data (RTD) commerce platform with four areas of emphasis:

1. Mobile optimization with CRM (Customer Relations Management) integration
2. Implementation of the Virtual Layaway platform, which is the next generation of internet-based Layaway software: http://www.vlayaway.com
3. Implementation of an email platform and auto-responder
4. Real Time Data eCommerce platforms, such as http://ConversionFlyBuy.com

By honing in on these four areas, a retailer will be taking the steps toward reaching the web-footed consumer that seeks what they sell.

**Once upon a time, businesses flourished without
any technology until…the tech evolution began
to flourish and impact businesses.**

Need some examples? Machines for factory automation, telephones, then credit and debit cards, then wireless card scanners, websites, mobile devices, wireless and cloud transactions, and mobile apps.

Were you paying attention back in 2014 when the greatest paradigm shift since the start of the Internet occurred? Mobile device searches surpassed the desktop searches. That shift has imposed the greatest mandate of mobile optimization of the current web-based world, and it is backed by Google. *If your website is not mobile friendly, you're probably nowhere to be found with Google search engines.* Everything is based on the Internet for connectivity, and the optimal retail strategic platform will connect offline products to online eCommerce sites, which, in turn, are connected to the various Social Media sites. Add in complicated accounting functions, filling prescriptions, insurance coverage operations, and various patient data bases and we see the need for the Internet is essential, and the software to make it all work efficiently is a requirement, not an option.

Acceptance of what is to be is key, particularly for retailers who need to join the e-tail world to survive. The tool that these businesses need is Virtual Layaway, because consumers are going to begin to expect this in the virtual stores they choose for business.

Virtual Layaway is the only create your own vLay page(s) for retailers that join the vLayaway Business Network.

Retailers love the dedicated webspace called vLay Pages, because they show the potential of their business. The pages are designed with a specific goal in mind: to also serve as another website presence for retailers. In addition, there are no licensing fees or start-up costs to the retailer if you become a life-time chartered member. This is smart business! And by offering this opportunity for businesses to take that next step into the future of commerce, success is on the cusp for many and has already arrived for others! It truly is a game changer.

More buying power for customers.
Businesses can create new cash flow-producing passive income.

New cash flow creators do not present such opportunities to the retail sector often, therefore it is a prudent business decision to embrace the vLay opportunity. A great retail challenge is to have inventory in place as business sales ebb and flow. This is challenging, particularly when seasonality makes merchandise hot and then cold. Ultimately, it leads to "out of stock" and "rain checks", which are linked to a loss of sales— sales every business owner ideally wants.

Retailers that can match consumer desires with inventory access will realize more optimal sales volumes. Virtual Layaway is the sleeping giant in the puzzle. Imagine…

As a business owner, you have access to a tool that allows inventory management to become a perpetual virtual inventory system that increases your ability to size scale inventory allocation and replenishment. All it takes is a single action—log into the back office and visualize new orders, due orders, and future orders without affecting the real time on-floor inventory. Next, plan by scaling up or down based on those real time numbers.

When business metrics are implemented the big picture becomes clear, making it easier to see which areas, in specific, are best to focus marketing efforts on. It makes sense, doesn't it? But unfortunately, this logical guidance is overlooked by many retailers—many of whom are on the brink of failing.

The goal of Virtual Layaway is to initiate a tectonic shift in the layaway business model and the consumer mindset—to think of layaway in the virtual transaction process.

This approach is a superior system in comparison to the out-dated physical layaway and warehousing methods of retail consumer products. More so, it meets the demands of our new world—a world that wants to conduct business virtually at an alarmingly increasing rate. It's not just appealing to those who grew up with technology, either.

There are a handful of major retailers that do offer layaway options, as we all know. However, they do not offer Virtual Layaway—something that is available 24/7—meaning that it fits for all people on all schedules, as well as those who are not near a retail location. Businesses without a layaway plan option alienate potential consumer purchasers, or place limitations on consumer product choices for a significant percentage of the retail clientele base.

Today, just as when layaway was first offered, there is a necessary procurement method for many families, especially during holidays and planning for birthdays. The smart e-tailer will recognize this and cater to this sales delivering convenience.

By using vLay pages, the system allows for flexibility for the customer in regards to how they schedule their payments and for how long. For example, in a retail setting if a customer sets up layaway payments for a 90-day period of time, the system is one that requires real time payout at any juncture during that time period, meaning that the retailer is required to have inventory in place for immediate or usual delivery.

When virtually offering products for sale, retailers have a value proposition in both real time online and offline. Customers can purchase differently, and from different motivations. "I really need this item, but I need to make payments." If a consumer is in need of a washer and dryer, but only has cash for one item, they can make better decisions. Buy the one that is most needed right away, and Virtual Layaway the other. It's a win/win for both, as the consumer purchased both needed items without high credit card interest and the retailer did not lose a sale.

Virtual Layaway **will:**

- Increase sales, cash flow, and profit
- Boost retail sales
- Decrease overhead cost for retail businesses
- Not require retailers to pull potential, immediate sale products from the shelves to be placed in layaway storage
- Allow retailers to utilize back office monitoring on pending layaway sales from initiation through final transaction of last payment—24 hours per day

Virtual Layaway **will not:**

- Require physical warehousing of products—the greatest cost to retailers
- Tie up cash flow in warehoused stock
- Create challenges from cancellation problems
- Prevent layaway of large items, because it is virtual
- Create staffing issues
- Lock businesses into prices
- Increase risk of product waste or damage

It all comes down to this reality:

There are only three ways to increase business sales:
- **increase the number of customers;**
- **increase the size of the sale; and,**
- **increase the number of purchases by each customer.**

Virtual Layaway pages helps to increase sales in each of these three ways.

Increased sales is directly linked to real time knowledge about the consumer demand chain. That's where it all starts for Virtual Layaway—which is just the beginning of exponential growth.

According to Megan Donadio, a retail strategist at retail consulting firm Kurt Salmon in an interview with ABC News: "When stores first started offering layaway again in '08 or '09 it doubled the volume of dollars of merchandise that is being bought through layaway." Why? Because it was a new income source. This is what Virtual Layaway is, as well.

There are over 28 million small businesses, each impacted and/or driven by the technological advancements that keep the business landscape constantly changing. That 28 million is the heart and soul of the United States economy, employing over 50% of the workforce, according to Forbes. However, it's only a minute percentage of that number that currently offers any type of layaway—they still think of "old school layaway." It's time to bring them to the world of Virtual Layaway, which is what we do.

Through tutorials, the software for success, and outreach to retailers we are changing the face of business in this modern world, taking eBusiness to the brick and mortar building in a profoundly effective way. Layaway isn't just for the "giants" – it is for every business who wants to have more sales. Don't miss out on your share of this untapped potential. Your business may be an eBusiness millionaire!

About Cassandra

Cassandra Backus is a native of Florence, South Carolina, and currently resident in Columbia, S.C. She is a Registered Pharmacist and a graduate of the University of South Carolina. Currently employed full-time by Lexington Medical Center, she has diligently worked third shift for 32 years. That dedication has resulted in the Lexington Medical Center Service Excellence Award and multiple awards for years of service. On a part-time basis she has been employed by Kershaw Health Camden, S.C. for nine years.

Education is a continuous process for Ms. Backus, as she believes the education process is never done. She completed and obtained certification from the Southern Institute of Real Estate, and is a member of the Association of Private Mortgage Investors. She has also completed study for the Commodities and Forex Markets. Those were past endeavors. Current endeavors that are pending completion is a Mortuary Science Degree from Greenwood Tech, Greenwood, S.C., and Market Traders Institute in Florida.

The last five years has been focused on Internet marketing and software development. As Internet business has taken hold of our everyday lives, Ms. Backus began to envision the future integration of the Internet into our daily lives and beyond. In 2006, when Wal-Mart made the decision to eliminate layaway services, she researched and read online how so many people were displeased with Wal-Mart for that decision.

Her epiphany and research revealed that making Layaway a virtual transaction would eliminate the problems associated with layaway, since the largest cost to the Big-box stores was warehousing cost. Paid products in storage for months, plus the cost of storage space, will debilitate the cash flow of any business. Subsequently, Ms. Backus began the process of software development for the layaway portal Virtual Layaway. The road has been long and hard along with the high cost of software development. However daunting, Virtual Layaway is finally ready to help consumers purchase more with less, and help businesses sell more products and services. But don't categorize this modern layaway for a certain demographic. Its benefits shall encompass luxury items to toys, business products as well.

There are multitudinous possibilities because it's virtual.

CHAPTER 22

OPTIMIZE YOUR OFFICE FOR SUCCESS AND PROSPERITY!

BY MARGARET M. DONAHUE

If the walls could talk, they'd have amazing stories to tell about the patterns and events that take place in spaces. Let's explore a few stories about the energy of offices and how it impacts the success of people working there.

William, a successful corporate executive, relocated his group to a larger space during a growth spurt. Selecting a window office for himself, he set aside an adjacent corner office to be used as a team conference room. In his office, William arranged his desk so that it faced the door. This contributed to a warm and friendly feeling as he welcomed people into his office. Shortly thereafter, William's relationship with his boss became tense. He felt unsupported and stabbed in the back.

It turns out that William overlooked an important detail. Although far away, William sat with his back to his boss. After William realized this, he decided to move into the corner office. This time he situated his desk so that it faced the door, as well as his boss. Almost immediately, things changed for the better! This one shift turned out to be a huge game-changer.

Elizabeth also knew the importance of creating a successful office environment. As director of a nonprofit organization, she spent long hours writing grant applications to secure funding. After trying multiple office arrangements, she discovered that she was most productive when her desk faced the door and there was a solid wall behind her. Stress increasingly took its toll, though, as requested grants were declined. Facing layoffs, finding money to fund the needed community activities became more urgent.

As she wrote her grant applications, Elizabeth missed some important factors that influence success. Clutter was everywhere. Paper piles, stacks of overfilled boxes, and little used equipment were tucked into nooks and crannies and scattered about. One of the showstoppers was two sets of file drawers stuffed with rejected grant proposals. Elizabeth didn't realize how clutter can negatively influence business. After discarding the applications and cleaning her office, income flowed again, and has continued for over ten years. More recently, this organization expanded into nicely renovated space and they are having a larger impact on their community.

In a third situation, Andrew's dream was to run his own audio business. His career and his passion were in conflict. After relocating his office to a huge bonus room above his garage, Andrew's business went south. Simultaneously, he was losing his hearing. Sitting with his back close to the entrance, Andrew's desk tightly abutted the wall of his small cubicle. It also was located near a steep set of stairs. If he wasn't careful, it would be easy for Andrew to inadvertently tumble down the staircase. Comfort and safety were not on Andrew's mind as he dreamed of his future.

Andrew relocated his desk to a far corner of his bonus room, placing it so that he also had a wall behind him and the large part of the room in front. Before long his hearing stabilized and he actively pursued his dream business.

Whether you have a corporate office, a home office, or other location, the physical and subtle energy of your work space directly influences your success and prosperity. The principles of feng shui provide an effective framework for understanding this, as well as providing a foundation for business success.

FENG SHUI PRINCIPLES ARE AN EFFECTIVE TOOL FOR SUCCESS

Feng shui is the ancient art and science of arranging your environment to enhance your life. It is about attracting positive energy to you and your business, delivering a high return on a minimal investment of time, money, and focus.

From a feng shui perspective, your environment mirrors what's happening in your life. Noticing the patterns and deciphering the clues can determine success or failure. The closer you are to something, the deeper its impact. The energy of the places where you spend the majority of time shapes your life the most. It reflects your energy and holds the patterns of what's happening. If you spend a lot of time working, then your office or workplace has a significant impact on your achievements and your life.

Feng shui teaches us that your surroundings are alive in the sense that they have a vitality that influences what happens there. Your spaces and possessions interact with you as they continually absorb the energy of the events that take place in each location, and then reflect it back to you in the events and activities that continue to unfold.

YOUR OFFICE REFLECTS YOU!

Fast forward to your office or work environment. The way you arrange and locate your desk, the quality of natural light, the wall color, the images, pictures, and symbols around you, as well as everything in your bookcases, file drawers, and storage closets, influence your work and its outcome.

One man I worked with was CEO of a company he founded. He sat with his back to the door in a sparse and cluttered office. He liked the way he sat and he had no desire to change. His Board of Directors eventually fired him as part of a "change in direction."

On the other hand, a woman arranged her office to suit her personality and please her heart. A black and white theme, her favorite colors, turned out to be stunning. In addition to exceeding her business goals as she embraced opportunities, many of her personal dreams have been realized as well.

OPTIMIZE YOUR OFFICE FOR SUCCESS

Four top actions you can take to optimize your office for success are to:
1. Create a clear and welcoming entrance.
2. Place your desk in a power position.
3. Eliminate clutter.
4. Connect your office with your work intention.

CREATE A CLEAR AND WELCOMING ENTRANCE

The door or entrance to your space is of prime importance. The objective is to welcome positive energy and encourage it to meander throughout your space. All entrances should be clear of blockages, squeaks, obstruction, and clutter. Doors should open fully and easily. All lights and doorbells should work.

If people visit your business, it's vital that your site is visible and easy to locate. Signs, flags, banners, flowers, and lights are excellent enhancers to attract business. Curvy paths encourage energy to meander to your business, bringing a more pleasant flow. If you work primarily over the Internet, the condition of your office entrance is equally important. A clear and open entryway helps you to develop and grow your business.

In another situation, a main door was obstructed by overgrown bushes, a broken light and doorbell, and a loud squeak. The woman had lost her job and wasn't getting a new one. She called the room she set aside for her office the "junk room!" After she trimmed the bushes, repaired the light and bell, oiled the squeak, and eliminated the clutter, she attracted a job. The physical obstructions in her environment had manifested as blockages in her life. Her new job emerged after she took inspired action.

PLACE YOUR DESK IN A POWER POSITION

A power position for your desk is one in which you can see the door, you're not directly in front of the door, and you have solid support from behind. A desk in a power position has the widest view of the room, as well as a view of the door, but isn't aligned with the door. The intent is to face the world to maximize opportunities and minimize surprises.

Sitting with a solid wall behind you provides strength and support.

Placing your desk on the diagonal with two walls behind your chair is empowering. Space in front of you allows energy to gather, bringing more opportunities.

Do you ever feel *up against the wall* at work? Check to see if this is how you are sitting as well. Creating more space in front of you can reverse this. Also, if your back is exposed and you don't have open space in front of you, you could be surprised by people coming into your space quickly and unexpectedly. You can change this by arranging a mirror to provide a view of the door.

If the door to your office is in the middle of a wall, place your desk so that you can see the door and you have support behind you. A plant, a low bookcase, or furniture can help avert an onslaught of disruptive energy if the door is directly in front of your desk. If you work at a computer, your monitor could also serve as support between you and the door.

ELIMINATE CLUTTER

Clutter is anything you don't use or love. We all have it. Some of us have more than others. In addition to visible excess, clutter lurks in over-filled file cabinets, stuffed bookcases, and too many electronic messages or files that aren't needed. Data comes to us faster than we can absorb it. Given the availability and low cost of storage, both physical and electronic, clutter accumulates quickly.

The problem is that clutter blocks prosperity. It can trip you up, cause one thing after another to go awry, drain your energy, stop you in your tracks, and bring your business to a halt. If it builds slowly, you become accustomed to it. After 30 days, you don't notice it. It becomes a part of you and your space. Meanwhile, you may become more stressed, anxious, withdrawn, or lethargic, or somewhere in between, without realizing why. Regular removal of what you don't use and don't like accelerates your success.

Clutter also hangs on your walls, particularly if you haven't updated your artwork in years. As you shift, it is easy to overlook the need to update your office as well. Stagnation results when you change and your space does not.

CONNECT YOUR OFFICE WITH YOUR WORK INTENTION

After your clutter is gone, intentionally enhance your office. Your wall color establishes an energetic tone; choose colors that align with you and your business. Place meaningful objects or pictures on your walls, and add items you enjoy or love. Fresh flowers, a green plant, a mirror, or something that reminds you of prosperity are wonderful office enhancements to support success. Note: you can have too much of a good thing. When it comes to enhancing and adjusting spaces, less is more.

The feng shui bagua, a symbolic map of life, is an effective way to boost office energy. Draw the shape of your office and overlay a grid of nine boxes, similar to a tic-tac-toe board. Lay the map over your floorplan, placing your office entrance closest to you, at the bottom of the page. Use the following chart to visualize how the energy of your office influences various aspects of business.

THE FENG SHUI BAGUA FOR BUSINESS

Prosperity and Sales	Fame & Reputation	Partnerships
Activate for flow of money, prosperity, good fortune. *Power Issues*	Activate to be more well-known or more publicity. *Stress/Burn-Out Issues*	Activate to strengthen partnership. *Codependency/ Overwhelm*
Work Community	**Center/Health**	**Products & Services**
Activate to strengthen connections. *Affiliation/ Connection*	The pulse of your business. Keep the flow moving. *Not being Centered/ Worry*	Activate for problem solving and more joy. *Stagnant/Limited Thinking*
Knowledge	**Career**	**Helpful People & Travel**
Activate for study, self-development, creativity. *Problem Solving/ Direction*	Activate to create more opportunity or a new job. *Listening/Self Discovery*	Activate for more help from others or travel. *Authority/Leadership*

Align with the main door or entrance along this side.

The nine areas of the map are:

Career: Center front. This area relates to your job, work, your career, your profession, and your aspirations. If you're in a job or career that does not inspire or motivate you, work with this sector to attract a position that is a better fit for you.

Knowledge: Front left corner. This area is about wisdom, self-development, and knowing what to do in life. If you need education or training to further develop your career or pursue a new one, energize this segment of your office.

Work Community: Center left. Your colleagues and the people with whom you work are your "tribe." This area is about employee relationships, motivation and teamwork, Human Resources, employee benefits, customers, suppliers, and the company history.

Prosperity and Sales: Left rear corner. This sector relates to growth, expansion, sales, profits, accounting, payroll, bonuses, banking, market share, and philanthropy. Money flows more easily when you show appreciation for your good fortune and you share it.

Fame & Reputation: Back center. This area relates to your public image. Integrity, illumination, brightly shining your light, and calling attention to yourself are a part of this, along with a clear vision, being reliable, visible, and portraying a positive image.

Partnerships: Right rear corner. This sector relates to partnerships, teamwork, inter-departmental relationships, customer service, shipping, and receiving. If you work for a subsidiary, keep this area in tip-top shape for success with the "mother" company.

Products & Services: Center right sector. This area is about the creative process, what you produce, and the future. This section relates to creativity, loving what you do, all communications, IT, remote offices, subsidiaries, and daycare. Do you want to have more fun at work or produce new products? Activate this area.

Helpful People & Travel: Front right corner. This section relates to the right people showing up at the right time, mentors, teachers, professional assistants, as well as seen and unseen help. This area influences key clients, financial backers, benefactors, vendors, suppliers, outside services, travel related activities, and community services.

Center: The center of your immediate space or your business. This relates to the core of the business, beliefs and values, the health of the business, employee health, company balance, harmony, product production, and solutions.

Whenever you're working on any area in your life or business, you can clear, clean, correct, balance, and enhance the related area in your physical environment. If you're looking for a new job or you want to recharge your career, beef up the Career sector. When you're ready for more education or training, set Knowledge in motion. Would you like more money? Energize for Prosperity.

Each part of your office holds subtle energy patterns. You feel these regularly, yet you may attribute them to "typical work stress." When the space is out of balance, issues emerge. When in balance, your environment supports your work or business.

OPTIMIZE YOUR OFFICE FOR SUCCESS

Let's face it: we spend a lot of time working. Now that you know the energy of your environment has a profound influence on your life, it's time to turn your office into a place where you thrive and your business grows.

If you're new to the process, take progressive steps to radiate strong, uplifting energy in your space and yourself. You'll encounter more rapid achievements after clearing obstacles. Claim victory for yourself and arrange your space accordingly. Optimize your office for success and prosperity today.

About Margaret (Peg)

Margaret M. Donahue helps individuals and professionals learn to live authentic, prosperous lives using easy, practical, and timeless methods.

No stranger to personal transformation, Peg has been following her passion and teaching others to do the same since 2000. Prior to this, she spent over 21 years in database marketing, working with large nonprofit organizations and Fortune 500 clients across a variety of industries.

Peg founded Feng Shui Connections in 2001 out of a strong desire to help people realize their goals and aspirations. Integrating a variety of tools and techniques, including feng shui, bau-biologie, meridian tapping, and coaching, Peg helps her clients shift energy from the outside-in, and the inside-out.

Since 2003, Peg has co-facilitated *8 Keys to the Ultimately Prosperous Business*, with Madeline Gerwick. This prosperity training program teaches business professionals and companies that energy management is the *true bottom line* of any business. Once organizations understand how to better utilize their energy and work in harmony with the Universe, they can prosper in any economy.

A graduate of Georgetown University, Peg also holds an MBA from Boston University. In addition, she is a graduate of three professional feng shui programs, the International Institute of Bau-Biologie and Ecology, and several coaching and intuitive development programs. A co-author of *Dorm Room Feng Shui*, Peg has also been an Adjunct Instructor in Organizational Leadership/Human Relations for Southern NH University (SNHU). In May, 2015, she received SNHU's Excellence in Teaching Award as an Outstanding Online Adjunct Faculty Member.

You can connect with Peg at:
- peg@fengshuiconnections.com

Her website is:
- www.fengshuiconnections.com.

You'll also find her on Twitter and Facebook:
- www.twitter.com/FengShuiConnect
- https://www.facebook.com/FengShuiConnections

Or call her NH, USA office at: (603) 537-9954.

CHAPTER 23

SEVEN SECRETS
– REDISCOVER THE GOLDEN KEY

BY JAMES N. SCHLONER

[Before I share this life-changing information with you, I just want to say I don't know just exactly what you'll find most exciting as you imagine how you'll be putting this to use. What's important is that as you continue to notice that growing excitement, you picture joining me on this journey of discovery. Have you ever wanted to find yourself learning life-transforming secrets? It really excites me to be sharing breakthroughs that transform people's lives. Tradition, Tradition, Tradition. We read the Torah today because the Ancients knew this secret body of knowledge. As you allow yourself to really tune in to what I have to say, you can find yourself being completely convinced for all your own reasons that this is truly important. J.S.]

My book, *Seven Secrets*, reveals how God's names vibrate in the deep Torah. The Ancients - the early leaders of Judaism - also held this same golden key to unlock the deepest secrets of the Old Testament, the Torah. What was the key, and what doors did it open? They knew two Torah's: one the written concrete Torah text with rules and commandments which we still know today. The second subtle Torah was oral not written, but magically lived at the heart - the depths of written Torah - magically lived deep inside the Torah because it vibrated with God's energy.

Here, beyond the stories surface meaning, the text pulsated alive like a subtle body. Like our concrete physical bodies pulsating with life-giving blood, the Torah's subtle body vibrates with God's names.

For thousands of years the best and brightest of Jewish tradition dove into this River of Divine Energy circulating at the heart of the deep text. What did they find there? Here, beyond ordinary meaning they had a close encounter of the mysterious kind, because here they directly experienced the beauty, majesty, and vitality of God. Lost your sense of wonder? Rediscover this teaching in my book, *Seven Secrets*.

DIVINE NAMES - THE FABRIC OF LIGHT

In the Torah, Moses meets YHVH (Yahweh) and comes to know his attributes intimately. Like the mystical school of Judaism - which structured the rules and regulations that today we call the Law - came to connect with God deep inside the Torah. Here, beyond the texts meaning they experienced divine glory which recharged their lives. In this regard, Nahmonides says, "We possess an authentic tradition showing that the entire Torah consists of names of God and that the words can be read in a very different way, so as to form names. Thus, the Torah as given to Moses was divided into words in such a way as to be read as commandments. But at the same time, he received the oral tradition, according to which, it was to be read as a sequence of names."

The rise of science in the last few hundred years has led to unimaginable advancements. Yet, the recent leaders of Judaism in an attempt to modernize the faith, purged the oral Torah from our knowledge base. This is like cutting the heart out of Judaism. For thousands of years, this spiritual heart animated Jewish experience. Nachmanades tells us the names are there but the details of this teaching were secret and not revealed publicly. Now, for the first time, buckle up and see the life blood of the oral deep Torah - the vibrant names of God vibrating in the text.

God manifests in the Torah through different "personages" and each has a different name. The four main names are Elohim, YHVH, EL Shaddai, and Eyeh Asher Eyeh. Each name has a specific unique quality. Elohim is traditionally judgement. YHVH is mercy. EL Shaddai is translated as Almighty God. Eyeh Asher Eyeh is the form of God closest to Being. It means I am that I am. Hebrew is unique because each letter has a number value. Therefore, each name has a numerical value:

Elohim	86
YHVH	26
El SHADDAI	345
EYEH ASHER EYEH	543

The Torah's view of names eclipses our modern notion. A name in the Torah is filled with potency and power: It is to know the essence of something. When Moses asks God to show him his glory, God grants his request because Moses has known him "by name." Likewise, God tells Moses the Israelites should obey his Angel because his "name is in the Angel." Similarly, turning points in characters' lives are marked by name changes: Abram becomes Abraham, Sarai turns into Sarah, Jacob transforms into Israel. Follow along as I uncover shocking secrets as you find yourself experiencing God's energy enlivening your every word. When God calls Abraham, he has to leave behind his ordinary surface life to reach the Promised Land. These names of God in deep Torah beyond the surface story are the promised land.

Let's look briefly at some passages and see this subtle Torah vibrating with God's names. The Binding of Isaac reveals specific details of this ancient secret teaching. God tells Abraham to sacrifice Isaac. The letters of this passage forge the surface meaning, but simultaneously the letters stripped of content tell a different story; Isaac speaks a total of 26 letters, the numeric value of YHVH. Abraham prepares to fulfill God's "Order" and speaks 86 letters. But these letters stripped of content also reveal God vibrating in the deep text. Eighty-Six (86) is the numerical value of Elohim. Also God and the Angel at the Binding with the letters from the name of the place, speak 345 letters, the numerical value of EL Shaddai. The surface text tells one story, and the deep text perfectly pulsates with God's names. Every Torah story vibrates in God's names like the Binding. Likewise, in Abraham's story, three angels come to announce the birth of Isaac. In this passage, Abraham and Sarah combine to speak 543 letters, the value of Eyeh Asher Eyeh.

Let's look at another two passages. At the sale of Esau's birthrite, Jacob and Esau combine to speak 86 letters, or Elohim. Similarly, when Jacob steals Isaac's blessing intended for Esau, Esau and Jacob combine to speak 345 letters, the value of El Shaddai! This subtle Torah forms a code, what I call the "Torah Code." This code is proveable objectively because it is number based. In my book *Seven Secrets Discover the Torah Code*, I reveal dozens of examples of this code animating the deep Torah. This code makes God look like a mathematician or a musician because the Torah vibrates with different names of God.

VIBRATING STRINGS AND SUPER STRINGS

The ancients directly experienced the essence of these different vibrating names, and so came to know God's qualities directly. The Torah is like a violin vibrating with different notes for these hidden names! Ironically, modern science purged this teaching from Judaism, but it is modern science that really is necessary to understand it. Quantum physics shows that creation is structured in layers:

- Organs Tissues
- Cells
- DNA
- SubMolecules
- Atoms
- Sub-Atomic Particles

The deepest level discovered by quantum physics reveals a world where everything is interconnected. The universe arises from this singularity or infinite unified field. This deep Torah resides right at the junction between the nothingness of the Infinite and the first impulses which appear out of nowhere. These names pulsating in the text are like violin strings.

Amazingly, quantum physics describes a similar structure to these vibrating names. They call them super strings. Vibrating strings structure the basis of the physical world like the names structure the basis of the Bible's stories. Lawrence Kushner in the *River of Light* discusses Jewish renewal in light of physics. He says, "Here is a vision of a new kind of physics working towards a 'unified field,' in which all the manifestations of reality are scientifically interrelated."

THE UNIFIED FIELD AND THE EIN SOF

There is nothing new under the sun. The ancients too knew an Infinite field at the source of creation. They did not call it the unified field or singularity, they called it the "Ein Sof," the One Without Limits - Infinity! They experienced this infinite fountainhead in meditation, by riding these divine names back to the source. Each passage of the text was a Holy Grail leading to God. Gershom Scholem discusses this doorway when he says, "There is an ancient midrash to the effect that anyone who spends the whole day reading the verse (Genesis 36:22) and 'Lothan's sister was Tinna,' which strikes the reader of the Torah as particularly meaningless and irrelevant, will attain eternal beatitude! The Kabbalist Azulai offers the following explanation of the aphorism: "when a man utters the words of the Torah, he never ceases to create spiritual potencies and new lights, which issue like medicines from pure new combinations of the elements and consonants. If, therefore, he spends the whole day reading just this one verse, he attains eternal beatitude, for at all times, indeed in every moment, the composition changes in accordance with the condition and rank of this moment, and in accordance with the names that flare up within him at this moment."

THE MEANINGLESSNESS OF REVELATION

Like Super String Theory which attempts to explain how the world was created. An early Jewish teaching, a midrash, says that "God looked into the Torah and created the world." The early Rabbis believed like Quantum String theory "The cosmos and all nature was already prefigured in the Torah, so God, looking at the Torah, would see it, although this aspect of the Torah remains concealed." It is this concealed teaching that my book *Seven Secrets* brings to light.

This teaching was the backbone of Judaism - its heart - for thousands of years, but it had become lost. Now, for the first time in hundreds of years, see what the deep level of the Torah the early rabbis experienced directly, intimately. They said the literal law was darkness, and this luminous divine fabric of names was brilliant light. They said, "His Torah is in Him ... and that the Holy One, blessed be He, is in His name and this name is in Him, and that His name is in His Torah." This fabric of light, fabric of names, is what they called the "Meaninglessness of Revelation." It is the story within a story - the essence of the text that led its seekers to a direct experience of the source.

The ancients believed in the power of the text because they experienced it directly. Rabbi Meir, one of the early Rabbis, talked about the potency of the text when he said, "when I was studying with Rabbi Akiba, I used to put vitriol in the ink, and he said nothing, but when I went to Rabbi Ishmael, he asked me: "My son, what is your occupation? My son be careful in your work for it is the work of God; if you omit a single letter, or write a letter too many, you will destroy the whole world."

THE BODY OF LIGHT: THE ADAM KADMON

We have been discussing how the names of God reside in the deep Torah, like pulsating blood, and Rabbi Arziel carries this notion further. He states the Torah text forms an eternal body with limbs, joints, and organs. These rabbis experienced this secret body of light in the text directly and this experience enlivened their health. They called this eternal body, the Adam Kadmon. Rabbi Arziel writes: "Just as in the body of a man there are limbs and joints, just as some organs of the body are more, others less vital, so it seems to be with the Torah. To one who does not understand their hidden meaning, certain sections and verses of the Torah seem fit to be thrown into the fire; but to one who has gained insights into their true meaning they seem essential components of the Torah. Consequently, to omit so much as one letter or point from the Torah is like removing some part of a perfect edifice. Thence, it also follows that in respect to its divine character, no essential distinction can be drawn between the section of Genesis 36, setting forth the generations of Esau (a seemingly superfluous passage), and the Ten Commandments, for it is all one whole and one edifice."

NEUROSCIENCE AND THE BODY OF BLISS

Deepak Chopra in his book *Quantum Healing*, describes two realities: Newtonian cause and effect characterizes most of the body's layers like tissues, organs and cells. Action and reaction - cause and effect - is like a bucket brigade, an effect is directly due to an observable cause. But at some level, cause and effect is not linear with an effect neatly and directly flowing from an observable cause. He discusses the subjective world of thought where a thought seems to emerge from nowhere. A thought is connected to the brain's messengers, neuropeptides. These fine impulses of matter flicker in and out of existence. What was the neuropeptide before it was a chemical messenger; and, where did it come from? Recently discoveries in neuroscience reveal that neuropeptides not only exist in the brain, but in organs like the heart, liver, and kidneys. This makes the body look like a "thinking body": a river of intelligence - a body of bliss, not a statue! This is what he calls the Quantum Mechanical Body. It is a body of intelligence existing right at the gap between physical reality and the nothingness of the unified source. This body of intelligence of bliss connects us to the finest impulses like neuropeptides and to the unified field. What is the source? An atom is 99.99% empty space. We are proportionally as void as intergalactic space! All the matter of the universe is made of atoms, from this vibrating, intelligent emptiness.

The early Jewish leaders knew this body of intelligence. They called it the Adam Kadmon. The deep Torah vibrates in a fabric of divine names - luminous brilliant light. This deep Torah forms an eternal body of light which is the basis of the physical body. Today, advances of neuroscience demonstrate how the subtle body displays a level of intelligence and organizing power unimaginable only a generation ago. Maybe the mystics were just ahead of their time. God wants us to know him. Come to know God directly, experience the magic of *Seven Secrets*.

About James

James N. Schloner has practiced law in Minnesota for 33 years. Mr. Schloner has written two books: *The Kabbalah Code* and *Seven Secrets Discover the Torah Code*. *Seven Secrets* is a rediscovery of ancient knowledge. The best and brightest Jewish leaders throughout the ages knew the secrets: James Schloner has revitalized God's revelation.

James N. Schloner makes it easy to connect with God's presence. Mr. Schloner has a unique perspective on the Torah because he has meditated for over 30 years. Let Mr. Schloner's experience ignite your passion for the Divine. Mr. Schloner is an advocate for showing us the hidden part of life.

CHAPTER 24

BECOME A "CONTINUOUS TRANSFORMER" TO BUILD LIFELONG HEALTH AND WEALTH

BY LINDA EVENHUIS

I woke up and made the commitment to become a continuous transformer. I think that is the best way to describe how I felt, when I started to accelerate my personal and career transformation for *lifelong* health and wealth. Have you ever felt that deep down you know that you have what it takes to realize your desired lifestyle, but you get discouraged by your own mindset and actions, and trapped in the same old story of your life? Avoiding eating those frogs that are holding you back? Wanting to do too much at once, and then just give up because things just will not change for the better? Knowing you *can* do it, however not having the right mindset and right formula to follow through on your road to success to lifelong health and wealth? That is how I felt. I kept on falling into the same traps (not exercising, not doing the work I really love, and not having a system that builds my wealth), before really breaking through in my "continuous transformation" lifestyle.

It is like figuring out your (mental) road map towards your life's destiny, and that takes time to figure out. It can feel like a constant search, there is so much contradictory information out there to attain health and wealth. Moreover, we tend to lead busy lives in a constantly changing world, and that could be one of the main reasons why people might be unsuccessful in their transformations. Because they do not schedule in time to sit back and think about their optimum lifestyle, work on a plan and commit to chase it passionately with consistent action.

Often things are "not that bad" in your life and you do not know "what is on the other side," so why should you transform yourself if you are not sure if you can attain it? And what is it like on the other side? You get no guarantees in life. What price are you willing to pay in order to get the prize? Amazing how just one letter in a sentence can transform your life!

I was stuck in my comfort zone, and knew that this was not the road to *lifelong* health and wealth. I was overweight, but I felt I looked presentable and had no major health issues. I felt tired though. I enjoyed working in the banking industry because I loved going the extra mile for my clients and contributing to building the business. I knew deep down that what I really enjoyed was motivating and inspiring others to get the best out of themselves; I wanted to become a trainer. Moreover, I was working for money, but instead I wanted money to work for me. I dreamed of setting up my own business with a passive income stream and unleashing my creativity.

So how did I become a "continuous transformer," gradually attaining the next level in health and wealth as a lifestyle? It was a commitment to be a lifelong learner and the willingness to go the extra mile beside my day-to-day life. My brother and I grew up where an entrepreneurial mindset was instilled – no matter what, you just continue to make things work. If you fall, you just get back on your feet and you find another way. And taking it step-by-step, chunking my life down to bitesize pieces as this was a mountain to climb! I had to find role models who already achieved what I wanted to achieve. So who are my main inspirers for my transformations? . . . Brian Tracy, Jack Canfield, Anthony Robbins and Robert Kiyosaki.

In their own way, they make sure that I follow through on my plans passionately by following their success strategies. In Jack Canfield's book, *The Road to Success*, I write about how I found my road map by applying the Success Principles. So how did I transform myself into becoming a successful trainer, getting my health to the next level and building my system of wealth?

I first focused on my career change. I upskilled myself, gained experience at the bank and visualized a cool, informal industry to work for, that better suits my character. I got more than I expected. . . I now have the honor to work for the coolest and greatest sports brand in the world! I currently work at adidas as an in-house trainer where I first won a Manager of the Year Inspiration Award for an innovative Retail University concept as a Retail Trainer for Germany, Austria and Switzerland. I currently conduct different workshops such as presentation skills, communication styles, business storytelling, conflict management, change management and team buildings. My customer satisfaction ratings are excellent. Moreover, I have been selected to be part of a work group that will create a worldwide concept on "Finding balance."

Second, I reinvented myself through sports and got fit by incorporating sports in my lifestyle. I wrote an article about this health journey on the adidas Group corporate blog. My trigger was to co-facilitate the "Fit to Lead program" for first-time people managers. What a game changer! I changed my eating habits, focused on drinking ionized water, scheduled in more rest and adopted an athlete's mindset to reach my goals through visualization with the Success Principles. My life is now a holistic approach connected to my life's purpose; I empower others to be at their best and want them to be whoever they want to be, not what their outside world is expecting from them. That means I need to be physically and mentally fit to lead by example which drives me forward. So I am not "ticking off boxes" anymore, anything I do is a holistic approach. With each action, I think what will be the impact. Does this lead me closer to my life purpose and goals, or do I drift away from them? And yes, I have moments too, when I let my inner child decide. I need that buffer to operate as I strive for consistency, not perfection.

Third, in my spare time, I am building simultaneously step-by-step my private project, "The Health Builds Wealth Club" to start building a passive income stream. Every day I am taking small steps to have money working for me next to my passionate job. In this project, I can unleash my creativity and truly be who I choose to be. So how do I define health and wealth and how is it interconnecting with my lifestyle?

- HEALTH is for me a vibrating energetic body, mind and soul that are conceived by daily success habits.
- WEALTH for me is to be grateful to have a healthy functioning body, mind and soul, have financial security AND being able to realize all the great dreams in my life.
- HEALTH and WEALTH are for me clearly connected together in order to lead the lifestyle I desire. Based on a healthy lifestyle I am building my physical, mental and financial wealth.

In the Health Builds Wealth (HBW) Club, my career and life's lessons come together. Being part of any physical health club, it is a social place where people connect and get empowered to keep on track of their lifestyle goals. My focus is on uniting like-minded people who want to achieve their next step towards a healthier *Body, Mind and Financial independence.* I offer to connect with people who are ahead of the game in order for people to step up their own game and break through any limitations that have held them back up until now. Dare to transform yourself, it is so worth it!

One of the biggest lessons I learned in my own "Health Builds Wealth" journey is to actively seek out people who are better than I am in a certain area and are already successful in what I want to achieve.

Just like in sports, there is always a next level to attain. And through the network I set up, I feel empowered and I do not have the feeling that I had to do it all by myself, there is always someone to empower me when I need it, Antonia Rodriguez-Evenhuis and Pablo Rodriguez-Mora, Krijno, Ronka, Dick and Astrid Evenhuis, Andres Cardemil-Mora, Ana Mora-Pedrero, Pilar Rodriguez-Mora, the Overmars, Nikitaidis and the van der Heijden family and friends Mia, Eva, Wynette and Nanci. Colleagues Matthew Stone, Angel Donchev, Alejandro Flores-Leal, Udo Müller, Manfred Echtner, Lea Musekamp, Falko Schmidt, Catherine Kraus, Laura Brandes and Gesa Bohn have contributed in their own unique way to get the HBW Club off the ground, just like many others that I thank in my blog. It is a true team effort. Dj Armin van Buuren, dj Tiësto and Guns n' Roses empowered me to keep on moving forward, music is uplifting!

Here are 10 tips that helped me to become a "continuous transformer", based on my own road to success that is part of my "health builds wealth journey":

1) Unleash your inner athlete and tap into the power of visualization.
Adopt an athlete's mindset and see, feel and believe you can achieve your future. Focus on the prize, not the price you have to pay for your sacrifices. Enjoy your journey! It is all about the person that you become during the journey. The toughest lessons are the best lessons to become the "you" that you want to be, challenge yourself!

2) Strive for consistency, not perfection.
I got a lot more relaxed since I adopted this mindset. I remember it was hard to get concrete with the digital road; I just did not look forward to getting started and wanted to get it "right" from the start. So instead of not doing anything, I just start to create and adapt as I go along. Just like in sports, there is always the next level and I let my websites grow organically.

3) Get a coach.
A coach empowers you to follow through and makes you reflect on your own actions.

4) Find role models to accelerate your transformational journey.
Thanks to Brian Tracy I am eating frogs for breakfast, I blast through procrastination and he inspires me in sales. Jack Canfield provides with the Success Principles a road map for my life and teaches me how to get to my destiny quicker with joy and gratitude. Anthony Robbins inspired me to become the rock star trainer and put my fear into power. I now turn learning content into an experience and create a positive and inspiring environment in my classroom. Robert Kiyosaki inspires me to have money work for me.

5) Focus on your own marathon.
Mind your own business. Often I see people who focus on other people, not on themselves. They talk about others, and blame their lack of results on them. Use your energy wisely and analyze what you need to change about yourself in order to reach your goals. Provide feedback to others and move on.

6) Live in the stretch zone.

Transform yourself to get to the next level. I see people building their "technical skills" becoming experts in their own "playing field." Great. But often I do not see them working on themselves, changing their own behavior for the better, open to new ways of thinking and working. Upskill yourself in your own personal development.

7) Be fit.

It all starts with you. You are the foundation for the rest of the world around you. In order to give energy to others, you need to have it first for yourself. I learned to keep energy for myself, which is not easy. It means scheduling "me" time first above time for your family, friends and co-workers. Lay comments of selfishness beside you.

8) Be grateful and feel blessed.

That is what makes up the quality of your life. Walk through life consciously. Remind yourself during the day what you are grateful for. Write your blessings down before you go to bed.

9) Commit and deliver.

Be selective in what you commit to. Renegotiate if you chose not to follow up on a commitment. This is the foundation of your reputation.

10) Celebrate your successes!

Celebrate those wins instead of ticking off your to-do list. It is the fuel that keeps you going on your journey. Enjoy life!

There is a wonderful destiny ahead, go chase those great dreams of yours!

About Linda

Linda Evenhuis is a co-author of Jack Canfield's book *The Road to Success* and empowers others to be at their best by designing and conducting trainings, workshops and motivational talks for the adidas Group and the Health Builds Wealth Club. She fosters a culture of positive empowerment and unites people in order for them to reach their highest (health and wealth) potential and meet their business goals.

She was brought up in a family that owned a small business where client loyalty, joy, open-mindedness and respecting each individual's life purpose were the foundation. The milestones for Linda's road to success were hereby defined.

Linda has a Bachelor's degree in International Business and Languages and communicates in five languages: Dutch, English, German, French and Spanish. To unleash her passion for Business Development and Relationship Management, she started her career as a global player working in the Fashion and the Banking industry. International Business, Account and Relationship Management positions were her main domain, where understanding and communicating clients' products, marketing, operational and financial needs were her key focus.

Moreover, she supervised contract compliance, negotiating payment terms, and ensured that payment, lending, investment and securities business was run efficiently and effectively. Conquering new territories through cold acquisition was another passion that fully goes with her determined and positive character, always looking for the win-win in a situation and entering unpaved roads to success.

Whilst on this career journey, she noticed she had a natural talent for empowering others and fostering a positive, goal-oriented driven culture. She started as a Retail Trainer at the Centre of Excellence Talent at the adidas Group for Germany, Austria and Switzerland, where she could combine her business and training skills.

There, together with Stephanie Dust, she co-designed and co-facilitated a new business demand-led Retail University program; an in-depth weekly Training curriculum based on her specialization in Emotional Selling, Customer Service, Brand Loyalty and Values. This was recognized with the Manager of the Year "Inspiration" 2013 award.

She was then promoted to Senior Manager Learning EMEA markets at the HR Talent Department, where she continues figuring as a key point of contact for the HR Community to build and deliver trainings and workshops. Custom made team buildings are co-designed with Matthew Stone. Linda is also part of the leadership team of the adidas Women's Network where she advises on the Training and Development curriculum.

The "Fit to Lead" program is one of her core responsibilities. Inspired by her own health journey, she successfully initiated a new Health Module focused on movement, nutrition, burnout prevention and a healthy mindset together with Lea Musekamp, Bart Groen and Ariane Reimer.

With her acquired business acumen, creativity, and passion for people, she pursues her road to success by managing her private business, the "Health Builds Wealth Club." There she focuses on a curriculum based on a "healthy body" through the alkaline lifestyle and ionized water in conjunction with running champion Gesa Bohn. A "healthy mind" is conceived by the *Success Principles* and "healthy finance" teaches how to build a passive income with ionized water and developing your own business.

- Linda@healthbuildswealth.com
- www.healthbuildswealth.com
- www.healthbuildswealthclub.com
- www.kangenwasser.de

CHAPTER 25

STOP MAKING EXCUSES
– START EMBRACING THE RIGHT MINDSET AND ATTITUDE FOR SUCCESS

BY TINA M. MEITL

You can have results, or you can have excuses, but you cannot have both.

The way we approach it all—good, bad, and indifferent—will directly impact our outcomes. Sadly, horrible things happen to really great people. I know that well, because I am one of those people. Life brought about a series of horrific and challenging events that were difficult and almost impossible to overcome, I said almost impossible! In fact, these things empowered me in a way that is hard for me to even believe at times, despite it being my own story. That is why today I have a motto, and it's massive: **Hear Me Roar!** Because if I can, I know you can and I did it. It just takes the desire to be Resilient, Perseverant and Intense with a Passion and Vision.

For me, honesty that isn't sugar coated along with a healthy dose of funny sarcasm are essential tools that helped me get from where I was, to the place I am now. Those same things will help me get to where I want to be, because it's not what you think you are that holds you back. It's what you think you are not. When I was growing up I had an average family, the oldest of three, and hardworking parents. We were "ideal" to many. Life was even keeled and non-eventful and I knew no other way. About the toughest thing I had to deal with was being so tall—5'10" by the time I was in sixth grade, and fully developed. It was awkward.

When I turned fourteen, something changed. The bubbly and outgoing girl that everyone knew became more quiet and introverted. They'd ask me, "Tina, what's wrong?" All I could respond with was, "Nothing." Because to the best of my knowledge, nothing was wrong. Somehow I had changed...overnight, really. My life as it once was, was gone.

As the years went by, I graduated, married and started a family. Things were "fine" by most outward standards and opinions, but inside nothing was right and I didn't know why. I started to look at myself in the mirror—really study myself—and I saw something horrible. I was fat and unappealing and felt completely worthless. And, oh yes, I only weighed 130 pounds. I was delusional, my perception of my physical image and the reality were at opposite ends of the spectrum. The mind is very powerful, it feasted and manifested itself on the negativity and inadequacies I fed it, amplifying the hopelessness and despair I was experiencing. I was on a wild roller coaster ride, mixed with all the emotions and unrealistic expectations of the disease. The momentum was gathering speed.

I spent so much energy covering my tracks, thinking I was so clever. You must understand that my purchasing boxes and boxes of laxatives at one time was a stunt act in itself. (WARNING: Do not try this at home.) I'd hide them in my pockets, my drawers, my car, anywhere I could. I'd take a laxative. If I was forced to drink water, I'd take a laxative to avoid that weight gain. I would "laxative" myself down to 100 pounds by ensuring that I was at a maximum calorie intake of 400 to 500 calories daily. I was anorexic and a laxative addict. All I could comprehend was that the image in the mirror was whispering to me, " Who's the fattest of them all?"

Then something happened that was hard to explain...

On my way to get a family photo with my children, I blacked out and passed out. Aside from it being amazing that I didn't drop my small baby, it was astounding that I did not die. I got back up and brushed it off with some quickly thought up excuse (I was good at those), but now I had a fracture in my thinking. In the back of my mind, I thought, *what if that happens again and I hurt one of my children?* It was unbearable to even contemplate. Finally, I realized I needed help and desperately. I was scared, irrational and out of control.

Nervous and scared as could be, I was at the Kansas City Medical Center filling out paperwork, questionnaires, and all sorts of information. They weighed me and I was only 98 pounds. Then they admitted me into the hospital and began to treat me with a "give her calories and help her gain some weight" approach. I was broken, mentally and physically. Well, I knew how to gain just enough weight to make my goals. This was advantageous because I could manipulate the system to gain just enough weight so I could see my children and husband. I was playing a game with my health, a vicious cycle of going round and round. I knew just how much weight I had to gain to be released. The first step in recovery is admitting I had a problem. Problem *not* solved!

Fast forward a few months...

I was back to where I had been and once again admitting that I did need help. I was to the point where I could barely leave my house because of the laxatives always being on overdrive and I checked myself into a different place in hopes of embracing the possibility of surviving. This place offered counseling, as well, so I'd managed to recognize that some help addressing my emotional relationship with food might be beneficial. Even in my perplexity, I was clearly not just physically unhealthy. It was larger than that. And that counselor, an amazing man named Jeff, found a way to tap into me and suddenly I was transported back to the age of fourteen. A mystery that was nearly a decade old was finally solved. I knew what had happened that had changed everything. I had been brutally raped by a family member. The experience was blocked from my mind and in hiding, because I wasn't able to cope with it then, but it had certainly wreaked some havoc on my life. But now I knew. I could start over and heal and become the person that I envisioned I could be, and my family certainly was desperate to find, as well.

I left that establishment with some parting words from the counselor: Be careful, Tina, because you have not hit rock bottom *yet*.

Well, I thought they were the ones with problems. How could I not have hit rock bottom yet? I was in a constant struggle with physical problems, emotional problems, and this anger that I needed to get over about what had been done to me. Now that I knew what had happened and those around me knew what I was up against, they kept a close eye on me. They'd let me know when I had my "anorexic eyes." Those are the same

221

type of eyes that you get when you go home and look at your pet and can tell that they've done something wrong. They look sad and their eyes are hollow. That was me, my life, my turmoil.

I knew that surviving moment to moment was my goal. It wasn't about even a minute, an hour, or a day. It was about that exact moment and finding a way to get through it.

I wanted to make it out of my situation. I was battling the rape, depression, and anorexia all at the same time, and it was intensely exhausting. There were no opportunities to just relax and go with the flow, because doing that could lead to a relapse. One day while visiting my counselor, I said, "I wish I was dead. I don't want to fight anymore. I can't do it anymore." No sooner than the words came out of my mouth, I wished I could reel them back in. It was like that little devil had popped onto my left shoulder and forced me to do it. I freaked. I ran. And that's when I got it…that moment was my rock bottom.

What I'd done was huge and I was so scared to go home so I took my time on the couple hour trek to my home, finally arriving six hours later and ready to go to bed. And when I saw my home in the distance I was relieved, until I also took note of the sheriff that was waiting there for me, holding a court order that said I had to go back with him. All I wanted to do was go to bed and forget it happened, but that choice had been taken away from me. I was escorted back to the hospital and placed on suicide watch.

In the hospital again, the therapy was more intensive this time because of the suicide threat, and I was also taking four different medications for all my problems. It struck me as strange on how none of these things happened because of the anorexia on its own. Because without a doubt, anorexia is a slow, painful form of suicide. But such as it was…there I was. There was a mirror in my room and I'd pass it by and actually see the fat on my body moving and attaching itself to me, horrifying me and scaring me, while also repulsing me.

But I had a plan…

They didn't really pay too close attention to if you really took your meds or not. So when I'd get mine, I'd slide it under my tongue and take a sip of water. Then they'd move on and I'd take the pill out. I saved it. And I saved a lot of them. Then one night I took them all. That was it. I'd had enough. I was done. Well, by chance, the hospital changed its night routine that evening and they found me before it was too late. There was a vast number of blessed angels around me and they were telling me that it was not my time. God had a better plan for me.

At that moment I realized that I had the power to change my destiny. My kids couldn't do it, the doctors couldn't do it —no one could besides me.

It was not easy, though, but my fat lady hadn't sung yet and today I know she's not even humming. So, if that was to be the case I was going to take control. I was not a victim.

The years began to go by and I had bouts where it was tough, but I remained committed. I'd be vacillating from an abundance of excitement one moment to self-doubt the next, but I found balance more often than not—moment by moment turned to minute by minute and so on.

Since then, I've survived breast cancer and had two major car accidents, one which leads me to a literal situation that is laced in that therapeutic fun sarcasm I do love. I quite literally have metal plates in my face and I know it when they are loosening because I start to get a headache. I will meet with clients and say, "I have to apologize upfront, because I have a screw loose." They'd laugh, I'd laugh. The reality was I did have a screw loose.

Let me tell you, between the accidents and the cancer, there is nothing left to do but laugh at the irony of how all these seemingly terrible things have helped lead me to where I am today, and have actually saved my life. When I had the cancer, the scar tissue on my chest from one of the accidents stopped it from enveloping more tissue. It was removed and it came with a bonus—an actual chest. You see, anorexia wasn't so kind to me in that way, either.

So, all these things were finally working out and I was finding my voice and I was starting to roar!

Realizing that I was given all these opportunities for life, I had some catching up to do and abundant trails to blaze. I started to share my story on the stage so people could hopefully be inspired and see that it is okay to laugh and accept who we are for what we are. We still have value. This realization also lead to me entering into the insurance market, and it's a market that has been very good to me. My hometown is small, but I tell you, it's my home and my location doesn't limit what I can do for others. That is a powerful message to have—and one that demands to be shared.

I have a voice and I have the right to speak...

Yes, my "Hear Me Roar" is inspired by Katy Perry's song, but I play it every single morning. It is my reminder. I remember my mission, I know my purpose, and I am motivated by it. I'm a survivor and I've developed what it takes to get where I want and use my adversities as my strength.

There are no excuses, only actions toward success.

I believe that adversities are put in our pathway so we can learn and grow from them, and that's the message I'm taking to the streets through my coaching and public speaking. It's so important to know. Negative thinking is a tragedy, too. It stops success and that's a travesty, because success is beautiful and comes in many forms. It means something profoundly different to everyone who takes the time to define their own authentic vision of success. With me helping them, we're going to break it down and get real. Then I'll help give them the tools to keep it real, because like I said, only we can really do it in the end! . . . Along with a lot of smiles and laughs to make the journey all that much more incredible.

About Tina

The energy and passion that Tina Meitl has for living life to the fullest is apparent in everything she does, whether it's on stage as an Inspirational Public Speaker or in her office, where she is both an Insurance Agent and a friend to her clients. Regardless of who she is with, Tina always has a great purpose. She wants to enable and educate individuals and businesses, empowering them through the development of a pattern of achievement, excellence, and success.

Tina often shares this message with others: "I live in the pursuit of the perpetual challenge." This provides daily inspiration for her to be the consummate professional that helps people, impacting the world by making a positive difference one person at a time. Through a compelling personal story, she is able to build a connection with people that lets them know that they have the capacity to make solid foundational decisions in their lives, while also finding the inspiration in their adversities to use as a catalyst in creating something superb.

As a graduate of American College: LUTCF and the University of Kansas Graduate School of Business, Tina holds her agent's license in Kansas and Nebraska and has received many accolades and honors every year since entering the business, including: MDRT, Life Rookie of the Year, Blue Vase, Blue Vase Elite, Heritage, Heritage Elite, All American, Super All American, Life Agent of the Year, and Pacesetters. All of these prestigious, hard earned credits come from her home base—the small town of Oberlin, Kansas. It's not where you are, it's who you reach out to that makes this all possible. Because, as Tina puts it, "Success doesn't just happen, YOU must make it happen, YOU."

When Tina takes to the professional stage, she has the chance to share her transformational message with audiences throughout the U.S.A. and even internationally. It takes just a minute in front of her to embrace why her tagline is what it is—Hear Me Roar! Now, she can add Author to that list of accomplishments. *Success Manifesto* is a book that she has written a chapter for as a co-author with Brian Tracy. In addition, she is also in the final stages of becoming certified with the John Maxwell Team. Further certifications include:
- GAMA International: The Essentials of Leadership and Management
- GAMA International and The GAMA Foundation for Education and Research: The Field of Leadership Series, *Building the Right People and Building High Performance Advisor Teams*

With a loving and supportive network of family and friends, Tina is always grateful for those moments she has with them, loving their company as much as she enjoys to laugh and connect with them. She credits their continued belief in her to her successes in life.

If you would like to connect with Tina, you can reach her at:
- Tina@TinaMMeitl.com
- www.Facebook.com/TinaMMeitl
- www.LinkedIn.com/in/TinaMMeitl.
- Twitter account: https://twitter.com/TinaMeitl